THE WORLD OF ...

# English
## Revision

Steven Croft

# Contents

# And your point is?

Some topics or issues provoke a lot of argument or debate, with people often taking opposite views. Each side argues their case, trying to persuade others that their point of view is the right one.

Wind farms are a hot issue. Some people are against the development of wind farms – particularly in areas of great natural beauty. Here is a newspaper article illustrating two opposing views.

## Wind farms: Clean energy or a blot on the landscape?

*By Lisa Richmond, Secretary of Green World*

The biggest threat facing the world today is climate change, brought about by global warming. Unless we act now, the very future existence of the human race could be threatened.

It is vital that we make a serious effort to move to renewable energy or we will have no hope of halting or reversing the effects of global warming. The result? Disastrous! Disastrous for wildlife; disastrous for the countryside; disastrous for the planet.

**What can we do to prevent such a disaster?** There are many things, but one very important thing we can all do now is to support the use of clean energy from renewable sources. Wind farms offer us one way to create this kind of energy and help our planet to survive.

*By Philip Shelley, Countryside Preservation Association*

Is global warming a threat to the world? Yes. Do we need to cut the amount of carbon dioxide we put into the atmosphere? Yes. Do wind farms provide us with the answer to our problem? No! Why not? Well, the simple answer is that even if we filled the countryside with

wind farms they could not even come close to providing us with all our energy needs.

**Use alternatives to wind farms**

The price of a scheme – which doesn't even solve our problem – is that some of the most beautiful parts of our countryside would be ruined. The impact on areas that rely heavily on tourism like the Lake District or the Highlands of Scotland would be tremendous. Why ruin our landscape by constructing these hideous monstrosities when there are other, environmentally friendly schemes that we could turn to instead, such as solar panels on roofs and tidal power?

# Arguing your case

The Key Facts below give different techniques that you can use in presenting an argument to make it more powerful. The writers in the newspaper article use some of these techniques.

Each part of the article highlighted in a colour is an example of a particular technique.

See if you can identify each technique and draw lines to match them up with the right colour.

Rhetorical questions

Repetition

Use of exclamations

Threatening disaster

Emotive language

Offering alternatives

## KEY FACTS

Techniques you can use to make your arguments more powerful and effective:

→ **Emotive words.** These appeal to the reader's emotions and make them feel strongly about something.

→ **Threatening disaster.** This technique – 'If you don't do what I suggest, something bad will happen' – can be very effective in adding weight to your argument.

→ **Repetition.** Repeated words or phrases will add emphasis to the points you make.

→ **Rhetorical questions.** These do not require you to give an answer – they are used to make an effect, and if the 'answer' is provided by the writer this adds to the effect.

→ **Exclamations.** These are used to add emphasis and effect.

→ **Offering alternatives.** By presenting different ways of looking at an issue or of taking action, you can sway the reader's thinking.

## • TOP TIPS •

When writing to make an argument, make sure you:

• organise your ideas logically
• present your points clearly

# Persuasive advert

## Every home should have one

**Fed up with pushing your heavy old vacuum cleaner around?**

**Tired of struggling up the stairs with it?**

**Frustrated when you can't get into those awkward corners?**

We have the solution to all your cleaning problems with the…

### AMAZING!  FANTASTIC!  INCREDIBLE!

…wonderful new **hover cleaner** from the world famous Shift It Cleaning Systems Limited.

The nightmare of vacuuming your carpets is transformed into a dream when you use the GLIDE EASY TURBO SX 7 POWER HOVER CLEANER.

The technology, developed by the Euro Space Agency to allow vehicles to hover over the surface of a planet and suck up dust and rock samples, is now harnessed for you to use in the home.

The GLIDE EASY requires no pushing or pulling – it simply hovers millimetres above your carpet. Increase the thrust and it will simply ZOOM up your stairs.

The hover facility coupled with the integral, super turbo multi-angled suction pipes give the GLIDE EASY a power found in no other vacuum cleaner.

Order your 7-day FREE TRIAL now – while stocks last.

Should you decide to buy – which you will – we offer a no-quibble money-back guarantee if you are not completely satisfied with your GLIDE EASY.

If you order within 14 days, you will be sent a set of accessories worth £150 that will enable you to use your GLIDE EASY to shampoo your carpets and polish your floors ABSOLUTELY FREE.

Be the envy of your neighbours and order now.

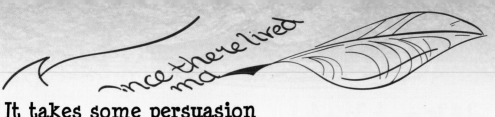

# It takes some persuasion

The leaflet uses several <u>advertising techniques</u> that make the message more persuasive.

Write down examples of these being used:

**1** exclamation ...................................................................................................

**2** repetition ...................................................................................................

**3** scientific-type language ...........................................................................

**4** a special offer ...........................................................................................

**5** emotive words ...........................................................................................

**6** a guarantee ...............................................................................................

**7** a rhetorical question .................................................................................

**8** status, to make you feel different from everybody else ..........................

## KEY FACTS

There are lots of techniques that make writing more persuasive, especially in <u>adverts</u>. Exactly which techniques you choose depends on what the writing sets out to do – its <u>purpose</u> – and the people it is aimed at – the <u>audience</u>. These are some of the techniques:

↑ **Have an eye-catching headline.**

→ **Use emotive words.**

↓ **Use technical language – often this makes something sound impressive.**

↑ **Use rhetorical questions to add emphasis.**

← **Appeal to status to make the reader feel important if they buy a particular product or do a particular thing.**

→ **Offer a guarantee for a product.**

↓ **Include specific details.**

↑ **Use exclamation to emphasise or draw attention to a point.**

← **Use repetition to add emphasis.**

→ **Include an eye-catching <u>image</u>.**

## · TOP TIPS ·

To make your writing more persuasive, understand the purpose of what you are writing about, and know the kind of intended audience you are writing for. If you use a range of different techniques that are likely to appeal to your audience it will make your writing more successful.

# Just like that!

Advice comes in many different forms, depending on the topic. At some time or other we all need to seek advice. You might want to know how to use your computer, where to find the right clothes for a special occasion, or the best restaurant for a birthday meal – the list is endless.

Here is part of a <u>pamphlet</u> that gives advice on looking after a pet rabbit.

## How to look after your rabbit

### Where to keep your rabbit

Rabbits can be kept either outside or indoors. If kept outside, you should make sure that:

- your rabbit's hutch is waterproof and warm
- it is not placed in direct sunlight
- it is big enough to give your rabbit space to move about
- it is high enough for your rabbit to stand up on his back feet
- it has a separate nest area
- it contains plenty of clean straw, hay or wood shavings
- it is well protected from dogs, cats and foxes.

### What to feed your rabbit

Rabbits are easy to feed. Here is some advice on feeding your rabbit the right kind of diet that will help to keep him fit, happy and well.

- Hay should form the main part of the diet.
- This should be supplemented with rabbit pellets that you can buy from your local pet shop.
- Small amounts of apple, cabbage and dandelions can be given, but don't give him too much or it may cause a stomach upset.
- Rabbit 'treats' are available from your local pet shop and can be given in small quantities.
- Make sure you control your rabbit's diet carefully as rabbits over six months old can often become overweight.

### Handling your rabbit

Once tamed, rabbits enjoy human company and attention, although you should always be careful how you pick your rabbit up. To pick up your rabbit safely, you should place one hand under his chest and forelegs and the other hand under his bottom. You should make sure that you hold him firmly but gently. NEVER pick your rabbit up by the back legs or the ears.

If you need any more information about your rabbit and how you look after it, there are good books on the subject, and you can search the internet using words such as 'rabbit pet care'.

## Advice made easy

Look at the leaflet again and link up the following features with the numbers for the appropriate lines on the leaflet:

- bullet points that make the specific ideas easy to follow

- advice on where to find further information

- clear title that immediately tells you what the leaflet is about

- short, to the point introduction

- sub-headings that make the structure of the leaflet clear

- imperatives that emphasise advice points.

**❶ HOW to look after your rabbit**

**❷ Where to keep your rabbit**

**❸** Rabbits can be kept either outside or indoors. If kept outside, you should make sure that:

- your rabbit's hutch is waterproof and warm
- it is not placed in direct sunlight
- it is big enough to give your rabbit space to move about
- it is high enough for your rabbit to stand up on his back feet
- it has a separate nest area
- it contains plenty of clean straw, hay or wood shavings
- it is well protected from dogs, cats and foxes.

**What to feed your rabbit**

**❹** Rabbits are easy to feed. Here is some advice on feeding your rabbit the right kind of diet that will help to keep him fit, happy and well.

**❺**
- Hay should form the main part of the diet.
- This should be supplemented with rabbit pellets that you can buy from your local pet shop.
- Small amounts of apple, cabbage and dandelions can be given, but don't give him too much or it may cause a stomach upset.
- Rabbit 'treats' are available from your local pet shop and can be given in small quantities.
- Make sure you control your rabbit's diet carefully as rabbits over six months old can often become overweight.

**Handling your rabbit**

Once tamed, rabbits enjoy human company and attention, although you should always be careful how you pick your rabbit up. To pick up your rabbit safely you should place one hand under his chest and forelegs and the other hand under his bottom. You should make sure that you hold him firmly but gently. NEVER pick your rabbit up by the back legs or the ears.

**❻** If you need any more information about your rabbit and how you look after it, there are good books on the subject, and you can search the internet using words such as 'rabbit pet care'.

## KEY FACTS

**When writing to give advice, think about the following things:**

↑ The writing should suit the audience and purpose you are writing for.

→ Your language should be clear and easy to understand.

↓ The advice should be structured logically, perhaps using sub-headings, to divide up the ideas into clear sections.

↑ If appropriate, imperatives can be used to add emphasis to the advice points.

← An indication can be given of where to find further advice on the topic.

→ Illustrations, diagrams etc. could be used to help make the written advice clearer and easier to understand.

## · TOP TIPS ·

When writing to advise, make sure that you are aware of the audience that you are aiming at and the purpose of your advice. Plan your advice carefully and use appropriate techniques and language to make your points clearly.

# Test your knowledge 1

1   Arguments often contain both **facts** and **opinions**.

   a)   What is a fact?

   .........................................................................................................................

   b)   What is an opinion?

   .........................................................................................................................

                                  **(2 marks)**

2   Write down alongside each statement whether they are a **fact** or an **opinion**.

   a)   Wind farms are a good thing.       .............................................................

   b)   *Coronation Street* is a soap opera.   .............................................................

   c)   *The Lord of the Rings* is a film.     .............................................................

   d)   Harry Potter is a fictitious character.  .............................................................

   e)   Smoking can damage your health.    .............................................................

   f)   Skateboarding is a fantastic hobby.  ............................................  **(6 marks)**

3   When writing an argument, what should you make sure your opening paragraph does?

.........................................................................................................................

                                  **(2 marks)**

4   Why might you use repetition in your writing?

.........................................................................................................................

                                  **(2 marks)**

5   a)   What is a rhetorical question?

   .........................................................................................................................

   b)   Why might you use a rhetorical question?

   .........................................................................................................................

                                  **(4 marks)**

6   What is emotive language?

.........................................................................................................................

                                  **(2 marks)**

7   Why are bullet points used in a piece of writing?

.........................................................................................................................

                                  **(2 marks)**

**8** Why might a piece of writing include a checklist?

.................................................................................................................................

(2 marks)

**9** Fill in the gaps in these sentences.

a) The function of a piece of writing is called its .................................................................

b) The group of people a piece of writing is aimed at is called its .................................................

(2 marks)

**10** Underline the words that can be used as imperatives.

stop        and        river        never        because        quiet

(2 marks)

**11** Name four examples of writing which might offer advice of some kind.

.................................................................................................................................

(2 marks)

**12** Name four techniques that you might use to help you present advice more effectively.

.................................................................................................................................

(2 marks)

(Total 30 marks)

# Do what it says on the card

Some types of writing give you particular information or explain or describe something to you. For example, a food recipe informs, explains and describes, in such a way that you are able to understand clearly what to do. Read through the recipe below.

## Sweet and sour chicken with egg fried rice

**Preparation and cooking time**
20 minutes

**Serves 2**

**Ingredients**
2 chicken breasts
1 onion
1 green pepper
2 cups of long grain rice
2 eggs
Small jar of sweet and sour sauce
Cooking oil
Milk
Pineapple juice
Salt and pepper
Spring onions
Prawn crackers

**Method**
1. Boil the rice until almost cooked, with grains still slightly hard.
2. Cut the chicken breasts into cubes.
3. Roughly chop the onion and green pepper.
4. Heat two tablespoons of oil in a frying pan.
5. Place the chicken in the oil and stir-fry until brown.
6. Place the onions and green peppers in the pan and continue to stir-fry on medium heat for two or three minutes.
7. Add the sweet and sour sauce and turn down heat to low.
8. Beat the eggs thoroughly and add a little milk.
9. Heat a little oil in a frying pan.
10. When the oil is hot, pour in the beaten egg and fry for a minute until the egg begins to solidify. Then, break the egg up into small pieces and add the rice.
11. Stir-fry the egg and rice together until the rice is completely heated through.
12. To the sweet and sour chicken, add a few tablespoons of pineapple juice and a little salt and pepper to taste, and continue to heat for 1 or 2 minutes.

**To serve**
Fluff up the rice and place onto warmed plates and flatten. Spoon the sweet and sour chicken into the centre of the rice. Garnish with chopped spring onions and serve with prawn crackers.

# Am I making myself clear?

Think about the recipe you have just read. Copy the following statements and add an appropriate ending.

**1** The purpose of this piece of writing is to .................................................................

**2** The audience it is aimed at might be ...............................................................

**3** A list of ingredients is given in order to ..............................................................

**4** The instructions are given in order to ..............................................................

**5** The language used is ...............................................................

**6** Headings are used to ...............................................................

## KEY FACTS

**If writing to inform, explain or describe, make sure:**

⬆ your passage is suited to your purpose and your audience

➡ the language you use is clear and accurate

⬇ your explanation is structured clearly

⬆ your information is presented in an appropriate form

⬅ you use appropriate language in the description

➡ that the writing is clearly and logically structured.

## · TOP TIPS ·

When writing to inform or explain, make sure your writing is clear and straightforward and focuses closely on the task or subject. Assume that your reader has no previous knowledge of the topic. Make sure that you explain any specialist terms, and use headings and bullet points if they help you to present your information more clearly.

# Whatever happens next?

Imaginative writing often takes the form of a story (such as a <u>novel</u>), a poem or a play. The purpose of imaginative writing is usually to explore ideas and entertain the reader. Here are the openings of stories written by Year 8 students.

**A**

Bang! Crash! Sally woke with a jump and sat up in bed. 'What on earth was that?' she thought as she switched on the light. She listened hard, but all was still and silent. Quietly she got out of bed, put on her slippers and went out on to the landing. There was no sound from downstairs. Trembling, slowly, step by step, she went down the stairs.

**B**

James was almost thirteen but he was very small for his age. He had brown hair and green eyes which almost always had a mischievous twinkle. He had an older sister, Toni, who was sixteen and a younger brother, Tom, who was eight. His father was a policeman and his mother a secretary at a local solicitor's.

**C**

The streets were grey and grimy and matched the dull grey of the sky. A cold and unwelcoming wind blew litter into the air and grit into people's eyes. The tall tightly packed buildings gave the street a claustrophobic feel and added another touch of ugliness to the scene.

# How to make a good start

Passages A, B and C each use a different technique to open a story.

Decide which of the numbered techniques the writer has used for each opening, and write down the letters alongside the techniques.

**1** The opening uses shock or surprise to capture the reader's attention. ☐

**2** An atmosphere of suspense or tension is created. ☐

**3** The reader's attention is kept because you do not know what will happen next. ☐

**4** There is a physical description of a character. ☐

**5** A detailed description is given of the story's background. ☐

**6** The opening focuses on the story's <u>setting</u>. ☐

**7** <u>Atmosphere</u> is created. ☐

## KEY FACTS

When writing a story you need to:

↑ think of a good plot or storyline

→ create convincing characters

↓ think about the setting for your story

↖ create a sense of atmosphere

↙ start your story in a way that captures the reader's attention

→ make sure your story has an effective ending.

## • TOP TIPS •

- Write in simple, straightforward language, much as you would use in telling a story aloud.

- Use direct speech to convey the thoughts and conversations of your characters and describe how they respond to each other.

# Well, I think that...

When you plan to analyse, review and comment in your writing, you need to think about how to present your own thoughts and interpretation of a particular issue or topic. You will have an opinion on lots of issues. For example, if asked for your views on school dinners, I expect you would have much to write.

Here is a short article commenting on moves to improve the healthiness of school meals.

This is a bit of a dog's dinner.

Which bit, and can I have it?

## Good school food needs more funding

The views expressed by a celebrity chef have highlighted some of the problems that surround the provision of school meals, but have also provided some of the possible solutions.

One of the problems thrown up is how difficult it is to provide healthy and nourishing meals on the pitiably small amounts that school budgets allocated to meals. Of course, many head-teachers wish they could provide more money for meals, but with so many other demands on their budgets, this often proves difficult. The second problem lies with the students themselves – even when healthier food is made available, most students reject it in favour of burger and chips or pizza.

On the plus side, though, it has been shown clearly that young people's tastes can be changed, and that when tasty and healthy options are provided, with time, effort and perseverance, students can grow to like this food, and will eventually choose it over the less healthy options. It has also been shown that such meals can be provided within a reasonable, although slightly increased, price per meal.

Whatever happens, things have to improve. What we need is more people to make the kind of impact our celebrity chef has.

# Pros and cons

Read the article on school meals carefully.

**1** Using a copy of the table, analyse the negative and positive points about school meals put forward in the article.

| The problems of providing healthy meals | The positive features |
|---|---|
| 1 | 1 |
| 2 | 2 |
| 3 | 3 |

**2** What comment does the article make?

**3** What does this show about the view of the writer?

## KEY FACTS

**When analysing a text:**

- ⬆ read the text carefully
- ➡ understand the purpose of the writing
- ⬇ identify the audience
- ⬆ make a note of the key points made
- ⬅ think about the ideas
- ➡ analyse what is being said
- ⬇ analyse the language the writer uses
- ⬆ be aware of differences between fact and opinion
- ⬅ express your ideas clearly
- ➡ support your ideas with references to the text using brief quotations where necessary.

### • TOP TIPS •

Adopt a logical approach to your analysis: support your ideas with references or examples from the text, and comment on what your examples illustrate.

# Test your knowledge 2

1   For each kind of writing listed below, decide which category in the table it belongs to, and add its letter to the correct column.

| Writing to inform, explain or describe | Writing to explore, imagine or entertain | Writing to analyse, review or comment |
|---|---|---|
|  |  |  |

A   A short story

B   Notes on how to mend a puncture

C   A recipe for lasagne

D   A character study of one of the characters in a play you are reading

E   The script of a play

F   A pamphlet on how to keep tropical fish

G   A piece of writing assessing the quality of a film you have seen recently

H   A poem you have written

I   The opening chapter of a novel

J   An essay in which you examine a poem you have been given to study

K   A guide book on your local town

L   A piece of writing in which you examine how language is used in a newspaper article

**(12 marks)**

2   Fill each gap with a suitable word.

When writing a story you need to:

a)   think of a good ........................... or ...........................

b)   make your characters ...........................

c)   make sure your opening captures the ........................... of the ...........................

d)   make sure it has an ........................... ending

e)   use a variety of ........................... to keep your reader's ...........................

**(8 marks)**

3   Below are some things you should do when analysing a text. Put them in the right order.

   A   Re-read.                                      ..................................

   B   Note the key points of content.                ..................................

   C   Identify the purpose and audience of the text.  ..................................

   D   Read the text through carefully.                ..................................

   E   Think about your response to the text.          ..................................

   F   Structure your ideas in a logical order.        ..................................

   G   Note down examples of language use.             ..................................

                                                              **(7 marks)**

4   Complete this sentence.

   When analysing the language of a text, you should pick out particular words and phrases and comment on their  ..........................

                                                              **(1 mark)**

                                                       **(Total 28 marks)**

# What a story!

Have you read a really good book lately? If you have, I'll bet it had some of these features: gripping opening, interesting characters, a setting you could believe in, some interesting ideas and a satisfying ending. All these features are the ingredients of an effective piece of 'prose <u>fiction</u>'.

There are lots of things to think about when writing your own story, but the first is that your opening must capture your reader's attention. Here's how Charles Dickens began *A Christmas Carol*.

Marley was dead, to begin with. There is no doubt whatever about that. The register of his burial was signed by the clergyman, the clerk, the undertaker, and the chief mourner. Scrooge signed it: and Scrooge's name was good upon 'Change, for anything he chose to put his hand to. Old Marley was as dead as a door-nail.

*A Christmas Carol*
**Charles Dickens**

Ask yourself these questions about a good story:

- Opening – Does it capture my attention? Why?
- Characters – Do they interest me? What do I think about them? Why?
- Setting – Where is the story set? Is it interesting? Does it convince me? Why?
- Themes – What ideas does the story contain? What is the effect of these? Are they interesting? Why?
- Ending – Does the ending of the story feel satisfying? Are all the problems sorted out? What do I feel about it? Why?

You'll notice that a lot of the questions include 'Why?' When analysing any prose, answering these questions will help you make your own story a good read for someone else.

Supper's ready!

That'll be for you, Izzy.

# A novel crossword

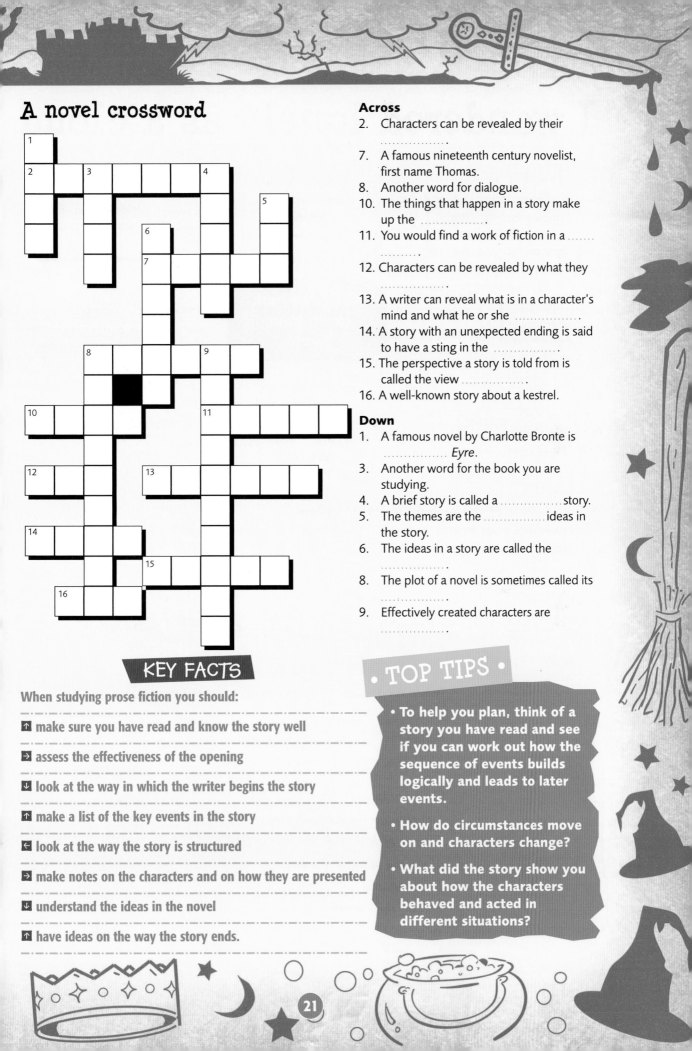

## Across

2. Characters can be revealed by their ................. .
7. A famous nineteenth century novelist, first name Thomas.
8. Another word for dialogue.
10. The things that happen in a story make up the ................. .
11. You would find a work of fiction in a ................. .
12. Characters can be revealed by what they ................. .
13. A writer can reveal what is in a character's mind and what he or she ................. .
14. A story with an unexpected ending is said to have a sting in the ................. .
15. The perspective a story is told from is called the view ................. .
16. A well-known story about a kestrel.

## Down

1. A famous novel by Charlotte Bronte is ................. *Eyre*.
3. Another word for the book you are studying.
4. A brief story is called a ................. story.
5. The themes are the ................. ideas in the story.
6. The ideas in a story are called the ................. .
8. The plot of a novel is sometimes called its ................. .
9. Effectively created characters are ................. .

## KEY FACTS

When studying prose fiction you should:

- make sure you have read and know the story well
- assess the effectiveness of the opening
- look at the way in which the writer begins the story
- make a list of the key events in the story
- look at the way the story is structured
- make notes on the characters and on how they are presented
- understand the ideas in the novel
- have ideas on the way the story ends.

## · TOP TIPS ·

- To help you plan, think of a story you have read and see if you can work out how the sequence of events builds logically and leads to later events.

- How do circumstances move on and characters change?

- What did the story show you about how the characters behaved and acted in different situations?

# I wandered lonely as a cloud

Sound effect, e.g. onomatopoeia – Bang! Crash! Plop!

Repetition, used for effects and emphasis

Vocabulary, the words the poet uses

Imagery, e.g. simile

**Things to look for in your poem**

Imagery, e.g. personification

Rhyme, e.g. rhyming couplet

Sound effect, e.g. alliteration – smooth, silky, soft

Imagery, e.g. metaphor

**Look at some of the techniques that William Wordsworth uses in the first two stanzas of his poem 'The Daffodils'.**

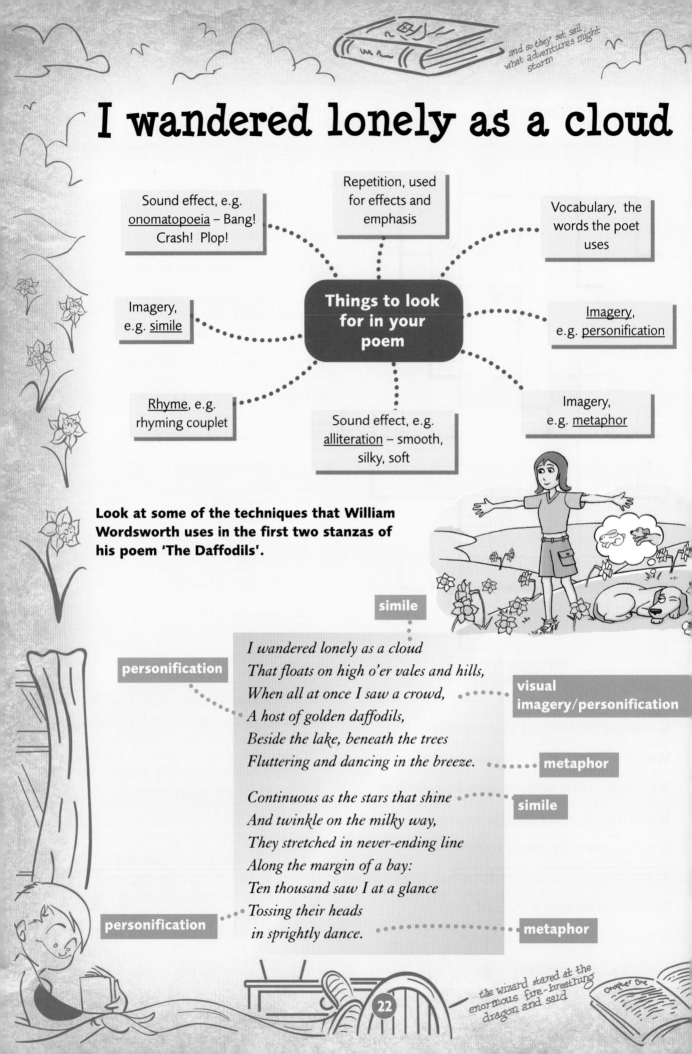

simile

personification

visual imagery/personification

*I wandered lonely as a cloud*
*That floats on high o'er vales and hills,*
*When all at once I saw a crowd,*
*A host of golden daffodils,*
*Beside the lake, beneath the trees*
*Fluttering and dancing in the breeze.*

metaphor

*Continuous as the stars that shine*
*And twinkle on the milky way,*
*They stretched in never-ending line*
*Along the margin of a bay:*
*Ten thousand saw I at a glance*
*Tossing their heads*
*in sprightly dance.*

simile

personification

metaphor

*and so they set sail what adventures might storm*

*the wizard stared at the enormous fire-breathing dragon and said*

*Chapter One*

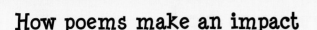

# How poems make an impact

Draw lines to match these lines of poetry with the term that describes each.

| | | |
|---|---|---|
| **1** | The wild wind blew, the waves grew high | |
| **2** | The cat sat hunched like a coiled spring | |
| **3** | The biting wind cut through me | |
| **4** | Clang went the bell, Splash went the anchor | |
| **5** | Onward, onward rode the six hundred | |
| **6** | Make but my name thy love, and love that still, And then thou lovest me for my name is Will | |
| **7** | The wind stood up and gave a shout | |

**METAPHOR**

**RHYME**

**REPETITION**

**SIMILE**

**ONOMATOPOEIA**

**ALLITERATION**

**PERSONIFICATION**

## KEY FACTS

When studying your poem:

⤒ Read it through carefully several times.

➡ Write down any ideas that come into your head.

⤓ Think about the ideas in the poem.

⤒ Look at the language the poet uses and pick out words and phrases that strike you as interesting.

➡ Comment on the effects created by your choices.

⤓ Think about the **tone** and **atmosphere** the poem creates.

⤓ Look for any use of imagery and comment on its effects.

⤒ Look for the use of rhyme and <u>rhythm</u>.

## • TOP TIPS •

The really important thing is not simply to 'spot' features but to say what effects they create and how they contribute to the overall impact of the poem.

# What a performance!

**This is how Shakespeare's play *Macbeth* begins:**

> [Thunder and lightning. Enter three witches.]
>
> First witch      When shall we three meet again,
> In thunder, lightning, or in rain?
>
> Second witch      When the hurly-burly's done,
> When the battle's lost and won.
>
> Third witch      That will be ere the set of sun.
>
> First witch      Where the place?
>
> Second witch      Upon the heath.
>
> Third witch      There to meet with Macbeth
>
> First witch      I come, Graymalkin!
>
> Second witch      Paddock calls
>
> Third witch      Anon
>
> All witches      Fair is foul, and foul is fair,
> Hover through the fog and filthy air.
>
> [Exeunt]

There are lots of things to think about while you are reading or watching a play, and your attention will be held if the play, like *Macbeth*, begins with a gripping opening.

Whichever play you are studying, it will contain a variety of **characters**, and you will need to form your own views of them based on a number of things, including:

- what they look like
- what they say (and how they say it)
- what others say about them
- what they do
- what they think (watch for <u>soliloquies</u> – they will often tell you this).

You will need also to understand the plot – the storyline – of the play.

# Witch scene

1 Look at the opening of *Macbeth*. Why do you think the play opens with thunder and lightning? ………………………

Complete these statements with your own ideas.

2 Short sentences are used to build up a sense of ………………………

3 Shakespeare uses questions to ………………………

4 Graymalkin and Paddock are the names of a cat and a toad. These animals are often associated with ………………………

5 Stage directions are used to ………………………

6 The lines are written in ………………………

7 These lines sound similar to a ……………………… that witches might cast.

8 This creates a sense of witchcraft and ………………………

## • TOP TIPS •

Always remember that you are studying a play and that it is meant to be seen performed on the stage. Try to imagine how actors might act out the lines.

# Test your knowledge 3

1   What kind of text would it be if you read 'prose fiction'?

.................................................................................................................................

**(1 mark)**

2   How might you learn about characters in a story or a play? Complete these:

a)   by what they   .........................................

b)   by what they   .........................................

c)   by what others   .........................................

d)   by what they   .........................................

**(4 marks)**

3   What should the opening of a story or play do?

.................................................................................................................................

**(1 mark)**

4   What is the 'setting' of a story or play?

.................................................................................................................................

**(1 mark)**

5   What is meant by the theme or themes in a story or a play?

.................................................................................................................................

**(1 mark)**

6   Explain the following terms:

a)   onomatopoeia

b)   alliteration

c)   rhyme

d)   rhythm

e)   simile

f)   metaphor

g)   personification

h)   vocabulary

**(8 marks)**

**7** When studying a poem for the first time, what is the first thing you should do?

.......................................................................................................................

**(1 mark)**

**8** What is meant by 'atmosphere'?

.......................................................................................................................

**(1 mark)**

**9** Complete the following sentence in three ways.

Writers often use short sentences to:

a) ...............................................................................................................

b) ...............................................................................................................

c) ...............................................................................................................

**(3 marks)**

**10** What are stage directions used for?

.......................................................................................................................

**(1 mark)**

**11** What is the name given to two consecutive lines that rhyme together?

.......................................................................................................................

**(1 mark)**

**12** What is 'rhythm' in a poem?

.......................................................................................................................

**(1 mark)**

**13** When writing about a character how do you support your points?

.......................................................................................................................

**(1 mark)**

**14** What do the following terms mean?

a) Exeunt          ..................................................................

b) Structure        ..................................................................

c) Soliloquy        ..................................................................

d) Stanza          ..................................................................

e) Plot            ..................................................................

**(5 marks)**

**(Total 30 marks)**

# Does it have to rhyme?

Many poems do not rhyme. Often, though, a poet uses rhyme to help to establish the overall impact of the poem. Poets use rhythm to help create their effects too.

In this poem, 'The Inchcape Rock', Robert Southey uses both rhyme and rhythm.

## The Inchcape Rock

No stir in the air, no stir in the sea –
The ship was as still as she could be;
Her sails from heaven received no motion;
Her keel was steady in the ocean.

Without either sign or sound of their shock,
The waves flowed over the Inchcape rock;
So little they rose, so little they fell,
They did not move the Inchcape bell.

The holy Abbot of Aberbrothok
Had placed that bell on the Inchcape rock;
On a buoy in the storm it floated
   and swung
And over the waves its warning rung.

When the rock was hid by the surges' swell,
The mariners heard the warning bell;
And then they knew the perilous rock,
And blessed the Abbot of Aberbrothok.

The sun in heaven was shining gay –
All things were joyful on that day;
The sea-birds screamed as they
   wheeled around,
And there was joyance in their sound.

The buoy of the Inchcape bell was seen,
A darker speck on the ocean green;
Sir Ralph, the rover, walked his deck,
And he fixed his eyes on the darker speck.

His eye was on the bell and float:
Quoth he, 'My men, put out the boat;
And row me to the Inchcape rock,
And I'll plague the priest of Aberbrothok.'

The boat is lowered, the boatmen row,
And to the Inchcape rock they go;
Sir Ralph bent over from the boat,
And cut the warning bell from the float.

# How poetry uses rhyme and rhythm

Read 'The Inchcape Rock' again.

**1** Tick the rhyme pattern that fits the poem.

ABAB
ABBA
ABCD
AABB

**2** What is the name for this kind of rhyme? ....................................

**3** How many <u>syllables</u> are there in each line of the first stanza?

........................................................................................

**4** Read these lines from 'The Charge of the Light Brigade' by Tennyson:

> Half a league, half a league,
> Half a league onward,
> All in the valley of Death
> Rode the six hundred
>
> 'Charge for the guns!' he said:
> Into the valley of Death
> Rode the six hundred

What does the rhythm of the poem remind you of?

........................................................................................

## KEY FACTS

⬆ Patterns can be created in poems by both rhyme and rhythm.

➡ Rhyme can create a 'musical' effect to the poem.

⬇ It can place emphasis on certain words.

⬆ It can link lines and ideas together.

⬅ It can give a sense of ending – the rhyming couplet is often used for this.

➡ The stresses and pauses of the rhythm can create a particular effect, for example create a quick tempo or a slow relaxed mood.

## • TOP TIPS •

Look carefully to see if you can identify a rhyme pattern and a sense of the rhythm in the poem. However, don't just 'spot' the rhyme scheme; try to describe the effect that it has on the poem.

and so they set sail
what adventures might
storm

# What is it like?

**Metaphors and similes are often used in poetry. Both metaphors and similes compare one thing to another in order to make the description more vivid. In this poem, William Wordsworth uses both metaphors (highlighted in blue) and similes (highlighted in red).**

*A Day Skating*
And in the frosty season, when the sun
Was set, and visible for many a mile
The cottage windows blazed through the twilight gloom,
I heeded not their summons: happy time
It was indeed for all of us – for me
It was a time of rapture! Clear and loud
The village clock tolled six – I wheeled about
Proud and exulting like an untired horse
That cares not for his home. All shod with steel
We hissed along the polished ice in games
Confederate; imitative of the chase
And the woodland pleasures, – the resounding horn,
The pack loud chiming, and the hunted hare.
So through the darkness and the cold we flew
And not a voice was idle; with the din
Smitten the precipices rang aloud;
The leafless trees and every icy crag
Twinkled like iron...

Similes are the easiest to spot because they compare one thing to another using the words 'like' or 'as':

> The boy was as bright as a button.
>   His hair was like mouldy hay.

Metaphors also create a comparison, but they are different from similes because, instead of saying one thing is 'like' something, they say it *is* actually that thing:

> The moon was a ghostly galleon
>   Tossed upon cloudy seas.

the wizard stared at the
enormous fire-breathing
dragon and said

Chapter One

30

# The same as or like each other?

Join each picture to its correct simile or metaphor.

1 My love is like a...

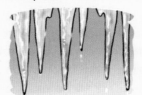

2 The hailstones were like...

3 You're as daft as a...

4 Your hands are as cold as...

5 He is as slippery as an...

6 This bed is as hard as a...

7 My face went as red as a...

8 It was travelling as fast as a...

## KEY FACTS

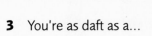
⬆ Metaphors and similes are two types of imagery.

➡ A simile always uses the words 'like' or 'as' to make the comparison.

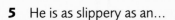
⬇ A metaphor does not use 'like' or 'as'.

⬆ Both metaphors and similes make description more vivid.

⬅ Metaphors and similes are sometimes used in prose writing as well as poetry.

## • TOP TIPS •

When writing about metaphors and similes, make sure you explain how the metaphor or simile works, what comparison is being made and how appropriate or effective it is. Always remember to use a quotation to support the points you make.

# Crash! Bang! Clang!

Have you ever thought where words like Crash! Bang! Clang! come from? Well, they don't really **come** from anywhere. Unlike lots of the words we use in English that derive from ancient or more recent languages, words like these have come to be used because they 'describe' sounds – each actually sounds like the noise it describes.

Bounce    Bounce    Squelch!    Bounce

**Whoosh!** went the wind through the tree tops.

The technical term for this is onomatopoeia. Onomatopoeia is just one of several ways in which you can create 'sound effects' in writing. Another effect is alliteration. This is when words next to or near each other begin with the same consonant letter. This technique is often used in poetry and other kinds of writing.

**S**oftly and **s**lowly the **s**nake **s**lid down the tree.

A third kind of sound effect is created when vowel sounds are repeated. This is called <u>assonance</u>.

The cr**ow**d sh**ou**ted l**ou**dly when the h**ou**se came d**ow**n.

# Sounds effective

Write down the effects used in these lines of poetry.

**1** Afr**ai**d, but br**a**ve, he entered the c**a**ve.

.................................................................

**2** **S**inging **s**weetly, **s**oft and **s**low.

.................................................................

**3** There was a soft **thud** on the stairs.

.................................................................

**4** The **r**ifle's **r**apid **r**attle **sh**attered the **s**ilent dawn.

.................................................................

## KEY FACTS

⬆ There are several key techniques that poets use to create effects through sound.

➡ Alliteration can create a sense of rhythm.

⬇ It can help create a sense of tone or atmosphere.

⬆ It can draw attention to certain words.

⬅ Onomatopoeia is used to create an impression of a particular sound.

➡ Assonance can create a sense of rhyme or rhythm.

## • TOP TIPS •

It is really important that not only should you be able to recognise these features in writing, but that you can explain the effects that they create, and why the writer has used them in the way they have.

# Test your knowledge 4

**1** What is rhyme?

..................................................................................................................................

..................................................................................................................................

**(2 marks)**

**2** What is rhythm?

..................................................................................................................................

..................................................................................................................................

**(2 marks)**

**3** Write down which of these lines rhyme.

A   Season of mists and mellow fruitfulness,

B   Close bosom-friend of the maturing Sun;

C   Conspiring with him how to load and bless

D   With fruit the vines that round the thatch-eves run

..................................................................................................................................

**(4 marks)**

**4** When two consecutive lines of poetry rhyme it is called a rhyming ........................................

**(1 mark)**

**5** What is a metaphor?

..................................................................................................................................

..................................................................................................................................

**(1 mark)**

**6** What is a simile?

..................................................................................................................................

..................................................................................................................................

**(1 mark)**

**7** Which of the following are similes and which are metaphors? Write S or M beside each sentence.

A   Plodding through the mud, his feet felt like lead. ...............

B   The mist rose like smoke from the valley. ...............

C   The cranefly's wings were tissue paper held against the light. ...............

34

D   The cotton wool clouds moved slowly across the sky. ..............

E   Darkness fell as suddenly as a curtain being drawn. ..............

F   The stars were silver diamonds shining in the dark. ..............

**(6 marks)**

8   What is onomatopoeia? Give an example.

..........................................................................................................................

..........................................................................................................................

**(1 mark)**

9   What is alliteration? Give an example.

..........................................................................................................................

**(1 mark)**

10  What is assonance? Give an example.

..........................................................................................................................

**(1 mark)**

11  Identify the effects in the following lines.

   a)  **Hiss** went the snake; **croak** went the frog.        ........................................

   b)  **S**lowly, **s**oftly, **s**ilently he **s**lithered.        ........................................

   c)  The thunder **crashed** and the lightning flashed.  ........................................

   d)  **Old** and **cold** the autumn grows.        ........................................

   e)  **B**attered and **b**ruised he **b**ravely **b**attled on.  ........................................

   f)  **R**unning, **j**umping the h**u**nt purs**u**ed.        ........................................

**(6 marks)**

12  Read the following poem and identify the features in bold.

   *The Eagle*
   He **c**lasps the **c**rag with **c**rooked hands; ........................................
   **C**lose to the sun in lovely lands,
   Ringed with the azure world, he stands.

   The **winkled sea** beneath **him crawls**;   ........................................
   He watches from him mountain walls.
   And **like a thunderbolt** he falls.      ........................................

**(3 marks)**

**(Total 29 marks)**

# Building the structure

Whether you are writing a story of your own or studying one written by someone else, the structure of the story is important. The structure is to do with how the story is put together – how it opens, how the events develop and how it ends.

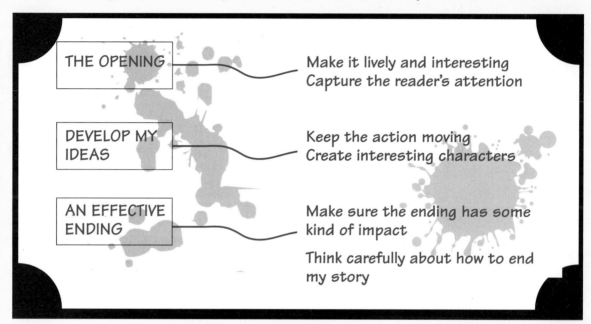

THE OPENING — Make it lively and interesting
Capture the reader's attention

DEVELOP MY IDEAS — Keep the action moving
Create interesting characters

AN EFFECTIVE ENDING — Make sure the ending has some kind of impact

Think carefully about how to end my story

## Openings

**1** The sky darkened rapidly and the ominous rumble of thunder could be heard in the distance. Things were looking black.

**2** 'Get out! Now! And don't bother coming back,' shouted Mr Smith at the top of his voice, his face puce with rage. Darren walked slowly to the door, opened it, took one long look back at the teacher he hated so much and then slammed the door with all his might.

**3** Sophie was a bubbly girl and was always so full of life. Her hair shone red in the bright sunlight as she walked slowly to the bus stop, her bag slung casually over her shoulder.

## Endings

**1** 'Well,' thought Jane, 'that's the end of that. I just hope that I never have to experience that again.' She shuddered at the very thought of what she had been through and then rose from the chair, looked around the room one final time, smiled to herself and walked out of the door without looking back.

**2** Harrison picked up the glass and gulped down the contents. Looking across at his victim whose glass already stood drained on the table, he smiled slyly as he waited for the poison to take effect on Clarissa. 'By the way,' she said, 'While you were on the phone I switched glasses,' she told him, calmly. He looked at her in horrified disbelief as he already felt the coldness creeping up his legs and into his body.

**3** It had been a beautiful day and now the setting sun drew it to a close in a fitting blaze of colour. 'Perfect,' thought Alison. 'It couldn't have been more perfect.'

# Unscrambling the story

Look at the following pieces of writing. They are all taken from the same story but are jumbled up. Number them 1–4 to re-arrange them in order to create a logical structure.

**A**  Looking back on the previous night it all seemed a bad dream. I lay back on the soft pillow, revelling in the soft warm sheets. As my senses awoke, the smell of cooking bacon drifted into my nostrils.

**B**  I slipped into the driving seat and started the engine. It seemed a lot longer than 48 hours since I'd been peering at the engine not knowing what to do. I revved the car and sped away, leaving it all behind me.

**C**  I knew that my luck couldn't last. I turned and saw two huge figures waiting at the door. Neither smiled. I knew this wasn't going to be a good experience.

I always knew they'd be sorry in the end. The problem with people who know it all is that they underestimate everyone else. I turned the key and opened the door.

**D**  It all began one dark night when my car broke down on a lonely road. All was going well until the engine began to splutter and cough and finally died on me. I got out of the car and lifted the bonnet, flashing the torch at the hot engine. Then the first drop of rain began to fall.

## KEY FACTS

⬆ To write a successful story you need to plan it carefully.

➡ Your opening should capture your reader's interest.

⬇ As part of your structure you should decide when to introduce your characters.

⬆ To keep your reader's interest, keep the action moving.

⬅ Make sure your ideas follow a logical and convincing sequence.

➡ Your ending should develop naturally from what has happened before.

⬇ Your ending should have some impact on the reader.

## TOP TIPS

You can end your story in different ways:

- You can pull all the strands together and sort out all the problems, or you can leave things unresolved – this can often make the reader think about what might happen next.

- Another effective way of ending your story is to have a surprise ending – sometimes called a 'twist in the tale' or a 'sting in the tale'. It completely takes the reader by surprise but logically fits in when you look back on the rest of the story. The famous writer Roald Dahl often used this kind of ending in his *Tales of the Unexpected*.

# What a guy!

When you are writing a story of your own, you will need to create some characters. Think about them carefully: if your story is to be successful, your characters need to be convincing. Here are two descriptions of characters.

**A**

He was a miser who hoarded all his money, giving nothing away, wasting nothing. His heart was as hard as rock and nothing ever moved him to sympathy or pity for a fellow human less fortunate than himself. When watching the news on television, even scenes of the greatest poverty and suffering left him unmoved.

**B**

She was a striking woman, standing tall, with dark wavy hair which shone a rich coppery brown in the sunlight. Her eyes were blue and were warm and friendly. They seemed to light up when she smiled and revealed her perfect white teeth. 'Hello,' she said, pleasantly, in a smooth, refined voice.

You will notice that these two descriptions use different techniques to tell us something about the characters they describe.

**A** focuses entirely on what **kind** of person the character is.

**B** focuses on giving us a description of the character's physical features – how she looks. You are given a hint as to the kind of person she is, too. It also uses some direct speech.

# Quiz-word

Use the clues to complete the quiz-word and find the mystery word.

| | 1 | | R | | A | | | | | | |
|---|---|---|---|---|---|---|---|---|---|---|---|
| | 2 T | | | | | | H | | S | | |
| | | 3 | | C | | I | | N | | | |
| | | 4 P | | | S | E | | T | | | |
| 5 R | | L | | | I | | | S | H | | S |
| 6 D | | S | | R | | | T | | O | | |
| | 7 O | | H | | | S | | | | | |
| | 8 D | | V | | | | P | | | | |
| | 9 D | | E | S | | | D | | | | |

1 When writing a story you need to .......................... your characters.

2 You can reveal your characters' .......................... and feelings in various ways.

3 Things can be revealed about characters through their .....................

4 You can .......................... your characters in different ways.

5 Characters can be revealed through their .......................... with other characters.

6 .......................... of how characters look and are dressed can be revealing.

7 What characters say and what .......................... say about them can be important.

8 A character might change and .......................... during the course of a story.

9 How characters are .......................... can tell you things about them.

## KEY FACTS

↗ Characters are an essential ingredient in a story.

→ Create characters that are convincing to the reader.

↘ Describe their physical appearance.

↑ Think about the dialogue you give them – what they say can give the reader important information.

→ How they behave in certain situations will reveal things about them.

→ What others say about them can be important.

↓ How they relate to other characters can be important.

# Where am I?

Another important aspect of your story is setting. 'Setting' simply means the background to the story or the place that it is set in.

The setting of a story obviously depends on what kind of story it is. Here is how Charles Dickens describes the setting for his story *Hard Times*.

**Use of colour**

**Use of similes**

**Use of smell**

**Use of metaphor**

**Use of sound and feeling**

It was a town of red brick, or of brick that would have been red if the smoke and ashes had allowed it; but, as matters stood it was a town of unnatural red and black like the painted face of a savage. It was a town of machinery and tall chimneys, out of which interminable serpents of smoke trailed themselves for ever and ever and never got uncoiled. It had a black canal in it, and a river that ran purple, with ill smelling dye, and vast piles of buildings full of windows where there was a rattling and trembling all day long, and where the piston of the steam-engine worked monotonously up and down, like the head of an elephant in a state of melancholy madness. It contained several large streets all very like one another, and many small streets still more like one another, inhabited by people equally like one another, who all went in and out at the same hours, with the same sound upon the same pavements, to do the same work, and to whom every day was the same as yesterday and tomorrow, and every year the counterpart of the last and the next.

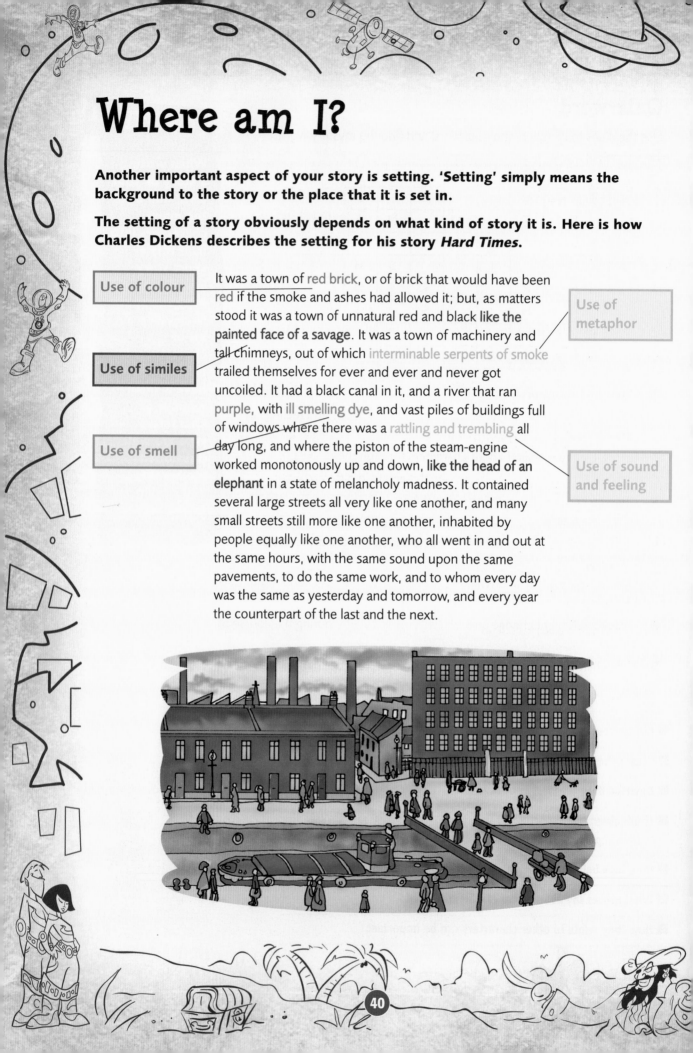

# Location, location

Link the following story titles with the setting where you think they might take place.

| | | | |
|---|---|---|---|
| **A** | Trouble in Year 9 | **1** | the sea |
| **B** | The butler did it. Or did he? | **2** | space station |
| **C** | Alpha 2 | **3** | a ruined castle |
| **D** | Reluctant Castaway | **4** | school |
| **E** | Jolly Jack Tars | **5** | country house |
| **F** | Spectres at Midnight | **6** | an island |

## KEY FACTS

↑ **The setting of a story is the background or place it is set in.**

→ **Settings may be taken from everyday life.**

↓ **Settings can also be drawn from the imagination.**

↑ **The setting of a story must be convincing to the reader.**

← **A setting can be closely connected to characters.**

→ **They can create a social context.**

↓ **Settings can be used to create contrasts with each other.**

## • TOP TIPS •

When writing your own story, use a variety of descriptive techniques to make your setting more convincing to the reader. A useful way to do this is to draw on your own real-life experiences – exciting or dramatic moments, people you have met or know or things that have impressed you. If you draw on your own experience your writing is likely to be much more vivid and 'real'.

# Test your knowledge 5

**1** a) What should the opening of a story do?

......................................................................................................................

b) How can it do this?

......................................................................................................................

**(4 marks)**

**2** When developing your ideas in a story of your own, you should keep the action

......................................................................................................................

**(2 marks)**

**3** What should the ending of your story create?

......................................................................................................................

**(2 marks)**

**4** A successful story needs careful .........................

**(2 marks)**

**5** You should make sure that your ideas follow a ....................... and convincing structure.

**(2 marks)**

**6** An important part of your story will be the ....................... you create.

**(2 marks)**

**7** Name five ways in which you can give the reader information about your characters.

a) ..................................................................................................................

b) ..................................................................................................................

c) ..................................................................................................................

d) ..................................................................................................................

e) ..................................................................................................................

**(5 marks)**

**8** Why shouldn't you put too many characters in your story?

......................................................................................................................

**(2 marks)**

**9** What is meant by the 'setting' of a story?

..................................................................................................................................

(2 marks)

**10** Name three ways in which you could make your description of your story more convincing for your reader.

..................................................................................................................................

..................................................................................................................................

..................................................................................................................................

(3 marks)

**11** Name two things that you can use to give you ideas about your settings.

..................................................................................................................................

..................................................................................................................................

(3 marks)

**(Total 29 marks)**

# In my opinion...

**Look at these two pieces of writing. They are both from magazine articles about watching TV.**

Most television programmes are complete rubbish, and watching them is a complete waste of time. All that seems to be on are reality TV shows, game shows or soaps. *Big Brother* is particularly boring, and I cannot understand why anyone bothers to watch it. The idea that television is educational is total nonsense.

Television can be very educational, with programmes that give you a lot of information on all kinds of subjects. For example, historical programmes tell you of events and people's lives long ago. Others on nature show you all kinds of things about birds and animals. The ones with snakes and spiders are the most fascinating of all.

When you read <u>non-fiction</u>, whether as newspaper reports, magazine articles, reviews or any other form, you come across all kinds of ideas. You can divide these ideas into two main kinds – **fact** and **opinion** – and as you read it is important to recognise one from the other. This is because facts give you information that is **true**, whereas opinions give you information based on someone's ideas or thoughts which may or may not be true.

One of the two extracts above contains some facts and some opinions, whilst the other simply consists of opinions. Can you tell which is which?

# Is that a fact?

Identify each statement as either fact or opinion.

1  History is boring.

2  Skateboarding is fun.

3  *Dr Who* is a TV programme.

4  *A Christmas Carol* is a novel.

5  *EastEnders* is a soap.

6  Blackpool is a lovely resort.

7  *Kerrang* is a magazine.

8  Hunting is wrong.

## KEY FACTS

↑ Facts are things that are true.

→ Opinions are the ideas or beliefs that a person might hold.

↓ Opinions may be 'true', but equally they might not be; for example, two people might have different opinions which are both valid.

↑ A piece of writing can consist of both facts and opinions.

← You should be able to recognise which pieces of information are facts and which are opinions.

## • TOP TIPS •

When writing a discussion-type essay of your own, try to balance facts and opinions. If it contains just facts then it doesn't really express your views; if it is all opinion then your ideas have no facts to support them.

# What news today?

The main job of <u>newspapers</u> is to provide news that we want to read. To make the news more interesting, newspapers use various techniques. Look at this report.

Eye-catching headline – note alliteration

Amusing sub-headline – note alliteration

## CYCLIST BUZZED BY BUZZARD

Bird bags baseball cap

A cyclist got the shock of his life yesterday when he was buzzed by a buzzard as he cycled home from work through a quiet country village. Nothing seemed out of the ordinary as Tom Treddle, 15, rode through the sleepy village of Pickern St. Mary yesterday afternoon. Nothing, that is, until a huge bird swooped from the sky, grabbed his baseball cap in its talons and flew away.

Sets the scene

Dramatic language

'I didn't know what hit me,' said Tom, 'It seemed to come out of nowhere, and I just felt the draught from its wings and, whoosh, it was off with my cap. I'd paid £12.95 for it, too.'

Use of direct speech

Bird expert Robin Rook told us that in his opinion this was an isolated incident and that the bird had probably been attracted by the bright colour of Tom's cap. Buzzards are large birds of prey and are quite common in the area. However, their diet consists of small mammals and they are of no danger to the public. Although not very tasty as food, Tom's cap soon made good nesting material!

Use of expert opinion

Details about buzzards

Amusing ending

# Read all about it!

Newspapers contain all kinds of news and information. Find 16 of them in the wordsearch. Some consist of more than one word.

| S | N | M | U | L | O | C | P | I | S | S | O | G | N | A | S | E | A | R | S |
|---|---|---|---|---|---|---|---|---|---|---|---|---|---|---|---|---|---|---|---|
| E | R | E | V | D | A | L | A | C | I | L | O | I | L | O | C | L | K | T | P |
| P | O | L | W | O | R | L | D | N | E | W | S | P | O | R | L | D | S | P | O |
| O | W | W | E | N | G | N | I | S | I | T | R | E | V | D | A | R | S | T | R |
| C | S | W | N | E | S | W | E | I | V | R | E | T | N | I | C | O | W | S | T |
| S | E | M | M | A | R | G | O | R | P | V | T | O | E | V | I | W | O | R | S |
| O | R | S | W | E | N | L | A | N | O | I | T | A | N | T | T | S | R | E | N |
| R | E | N | T | E | R | T | A | I | N | M | E | N | T | L | I | S | S | T | E |
| O | S | P | C | S | W | E | I | V | E | R | M | L | I | F | L | O | C | T | W |
| H | U | M | A | N | I | N | T | E | R | E | S | T | S | T | O | R | I | E | S |
| R | A | H | S | E | G | A | P | M | E | L | B | O | R | P | P | C | Y | L | H |
| S | H | L | O | C | A | L | N | E | W | S | T | V | P | P | R | O | G | M | S |

# Can you believe it?

**Look at these advertisements for a new flat screen TV and work out how each one attempts to make you want to buy the TV.**

The **ULTIMATE** in TV technology

The Xtronic 27TXi Flat screen TV and DVD player gives you advanced technology at its **BEST. Scientists have worked for years on the black atom crystal particle technology originally developed for space satellites. Now you can have it in your lounge!**

The Xtronic 27TXi Flat screen TV and DVD player comes with an unconditional **25-YEAR GUARANTEE.**

No other TV can give you such **amazing** images or easy control as the 27TXi. The picture is **fantastic** and far **superior** to any other TV in existence. It's simply **years ahead of its time**.

**Order today and you will receive a selection of 24 top-selling DVDs worth £200 to add to your collection - ABSOLUTELY FREE**

We encounter advertising every day in all kinds of different ways – television, magazines, newspapers, billboards and radio to name only a few.  The main thing that adverts try to do is to **persuade** you in some way – to buy something, do something, think something.

Did you spot the techniques used in the advertisements above?

48

# The language of advertising

Crossword grid with the central column spelling vertically: L A N G U A G E

1. Advertisements often begin with eye-catching .........................

2. A shortened form of the word advertisement.

3. Imperatives give ......................... and are often used in advertisements.

4. Adverts often give a ......................... on the product they are trying to persuade you to buy.

5. Advertisements often use ......................... to create a visual effect.

6. Catchy phrases are called .........................

7. Sometimes free ......................... are offered to try to persuade you to buy a product.

8. People who buy things are called ......................... .

## KEY FACTS

Adverts can be used to promote many things – holidays, charities, selling products, political parties, public information, jobs etc.

Adverts can use the following techniques:

⬆ exaggeration – claims to be the 'best', 'most advanced' etc.

➡ commands – 'Buy Now!', 'Stop and Think'

⬇ repetition

⬆ appealing words

⬅ words that appeal to the senses – 'tangy', 'tasty'

➡ sound effects – e.g. alliteration

⬇ humour.

## • TOP TIPS •

When analysing an advert, be aware of the purpose and audience of the advertisement, discuss the visual effects being used, examine the language used and assess and comment on the overall impact.

# Test your knowledge 6

**1** What are 'facts'?

.......................................................................................................................................

**(1 mark)**

**2** What are 'opinions'?

.......................................................................................................................................

**(1 mark)**

**3** Which of these are facts (F) and which opinions (O)?

    A   Manchester United are certain to win the League Championship next season. ................

    B   The lead singer's new hairstyle led to thousands of his fans copying it. ......................

    C   Cycling is good for your health. ........................

    D   *Dr Who* is an excellent and exciting TV progamme. ......................

    E   Skateboarders are a real nuisance. ........................

    F   Hunting has now been banned. ........................

**(6 marks)**

**4** What is the main function of a newspaper?

.......................................................................................................................................

**(1 mark)**

**5** Name four kinds of news that a newspaper might report on.

.......................................................................................................................................

.......................................................................................................................................

.......................................................................................................................................

.......................................................................................................................................

**(4 marks)**

**6** Give two things a newspaper might do as well as reporting news.

.......................................................................................................................................

.......................................................................................................................................

**(1 mark)**

**7** Why would a headline be used?

.......................................................................................................................................

**(1 mark)**

**8** What is a caption?

................................................................................................................
**(1 mark)**

**9** Why might photographs be included?

................................................................................................................
**(1 mark)**

**10** Name three things you might look at when analysing a newspaper article.

................................................................................................................

................................................................................................................

................................................................................................................
**(3 mark)**

**11** When analysing an advertisement you should begin by thinking about its .........................
and ........................
**(1 mark)**

**12** Name four places you might see advertisements.

........................ ........................ ........................ ........................
**(4 mark)**

**13** What is the main purpose of most adverts?

................................................................................................................
**(1 mark)**

**14** Name two visual techniques that might be used in adverts.

........................ ........................
**(2 marks)**

**15** Name two language techniques that might be used in adverts.

........................ ........................
**(2 marks)**

**(Total 30 marks)**

# What did you think of it?

You will come across <u>reviews</u> all the time in one form or another. A reviewer examines something, tests something, listens to or watches something, and then gives an opinion on it. Reviews can be about a variety of things, such as films, books, plays, TV programmes or music albums and just about any thing that you might want to buy.

Here's a review of the film *The Hitchhiker's Guide to the Galaxy*.

Did I switch off the electric blanket?

**A**rthur Dent (played by Martin Freeman) wakes up one day to find that his home is going to be bulldozed to make way for a motorway. As if this isn't bad enough, he then finds out from his friend Ford Prefect that the Earth itself is going to be demolished to make way for an intergalactic bypass. The only chance for survival that Arthur has is to hitch a ride on a passing spacecraft. This is exactly what he and Ford Prefect do – they stow away on a spaceship and escape just as the Earth is blown to pieces. But this is only the start of their adventures. To find out the rest you'll have to see the film.

The acting's great – Sam Rockwell is hilarious as Zaphod Beeblebrox and Bill Nighy is great as Slartibartfast. The special effects and camera work are outstanding, too – there are some incredible shots. It's amazing what modern technology can do to make you believe it's real. I can guarantee you won't want to move from your seat until the final credits roll.

I can't wait for the sequel. I hear they're working on it already.

# Convinced?

These sentences are taken from various reviews. Look at the pictures and link each one to the appropriate review.

**1** The quality of the sound is absolutely amazing.

**2** You will find it hard to improve on the brightness and clarity of the picture.

**3** Once you've experience the superb facilities here you'll want to keep coming back – again and again.

**4** Your carpets will never have been cleaner.

**5** Once you start this you'll not put it down until you have finished the last chapter.

**6** You'll find this one really bursts on your taste buds.

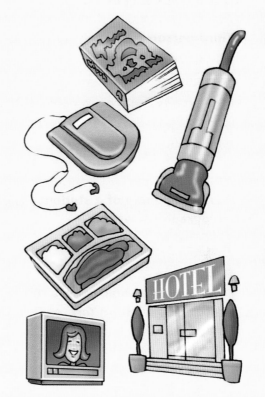

## KEY FACTS

A review gives an opinion or assessment of something.

When reading a review you need to:

➤ identify what view the review is putting forward

➤ identify how the review uses language

➤ analyse the effects created by the review.

## · TOP TIPS ·

Before writing your own review you should first think about the purpose and audience and be clear about your own view. Plan the review carefully, understand the difference between fact and opinion, structure your ideas in a logical way and make specific comments rather than vague generalisations.

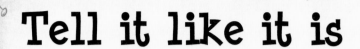

# Tell it like it is

**This is the opening of a student's piece of biographical writing on Shakespeare.**

### Third person

William Shakespeare was born in 1564 in Stratford-upon-Avon. His father, John Shakespeare, was a glove-maker and a prominent person in Stratford, becoming a manager in 1568. William went to the grammar school in Stratford and probably left school at the age of fourteen, which was usual in those days. In 1582 he married Anne Hathaway, the daughter of a local farmer.

**This is the opening of a student's piece of autobiographical writing.**

### First person

I was born in a small market town called Malton, not far from York, on 7 September 1991. I have three older sisters and even though I'm fourteen now they still treat me like their 'baby brother'. When I was three, my mum took me to the local toddler group but I must admit I don't remember much of that. My first real memory of school is my first day at the Infant School – memorable because I spilt a pot of glue all over the teacher.

A biography is a piece of writing that tells us about the life of another person. These are usually written by someone who has studied or knows something about the life of the person they are writing about.

An autobiography is also a piece of writing about the life of a person, but is written by the person themselves. Although similar in some ways, the style of a biography and an autobiography does differ. One way they differ is that a biography is told in the <u>third person</u> and an autobiography is told in the <u>first person</u>.

# Fill in the gaps

Complete the sentences with the correct words.

**1** When writing an autobiography you would use the ........................ person.

**2** A biography is written in the ........................ person.

**3** Direct ........................ can be used to bring the story to life.

**4** In an autobiography the writer is able to share his or her ........................ and ........................ with the reader.

**5** When writing your autobiography, your opening sentence should capture the ........................ and ........................ of the reader.

**6** In a biography, the writer might use ........................ from other people to describe the subject.

**7** A biography will give you lots of ........................ about the subject's life.

**8** When writing your autobiography you should concentrate on ........................ incidents and experiences from your life.

## KEY FACTS

⬆ A biography presents the writer's own view of the subject.

⬅ Autobiographies present a view that the writer wants to give the reader.

➡ They both describe events.

⬇ Biographies can give a more detailed or objective account than autobiographies

⬆ Autobiographies are more personal.

## TOP TIPS

When writing your own autobiography, address your audience directly and explain your feelings to the reader. Use first-person pronouns to express your ideas, thoughts and feelings. Some direct speech can be useful in helping to bring your narrative to life, but don't overdo it.

# What a shot!

Film and TV programmes are made up of a series of 'moving images' or camera <u>shots</u> that, when seen in very rapid sequence, create a lifelike impression of events taking place. Camera shots can be taken in different ways and from different angles. They have different names:

Long shot – sets the scene

Close up – allows us to see a face clearly

High angle shot

Low angle shot – gives a different view

# Crossword

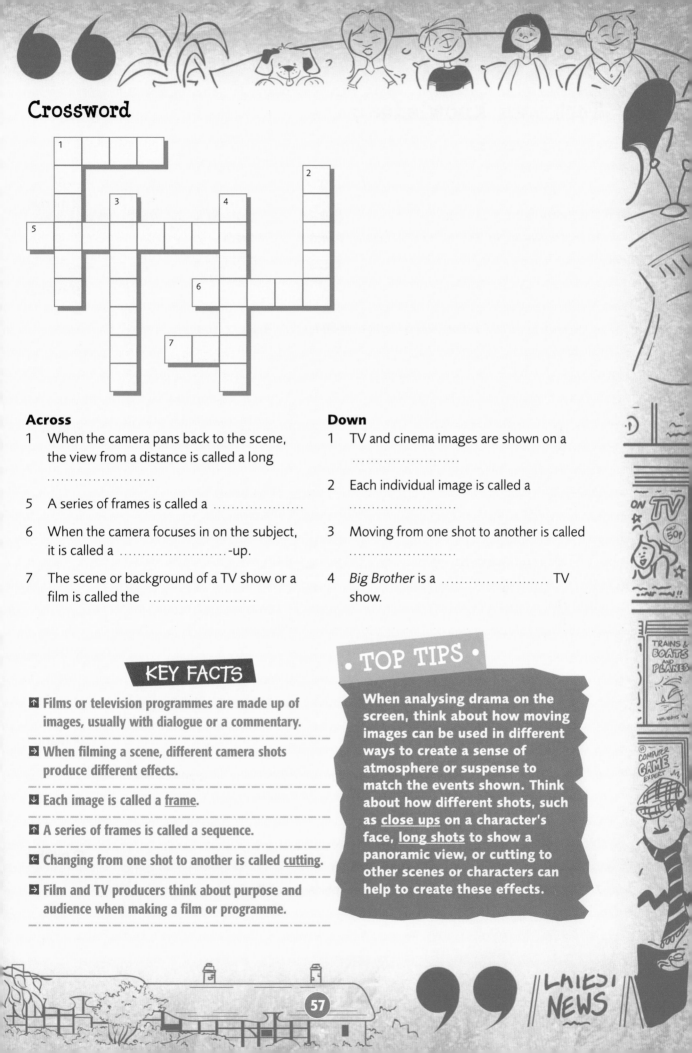

## Across

1  When the camera pans back to the scene, the view from a distance is called a long ........................

5  A series of frames is called a ....................

6  When the camera focuses in on the subject, it is called a ........................-up.

7  The scene or background of a TV show or a film is called the ........................

## Down

1  TV and cinema images are shown on a ........................

2  Each individual image is called a ........................

3  Moving from one shot to another is called ........................

4  *Big Brother* is a ........................ TV show.

## KEY FACTS

⬆ Films or television programmes are made up of images, usually with dialogue or a commentary.

➡ When filming a scene, different camera shots produce different effects.

⬇ Each image is called a frame.

⬆ A series of frames is called a sequence.

⬅ Changing from one shot to another is called cutting.

➡ Film and TV producers think about purpose and audience when making a film or programme.

## • TOP TIPS •

When analysing drama on the screen, think about how moving images can be used in different ways to create a sense of atmosphere or suspense to match the events shown. Think about how different shots, such as close ups on a character's face, long shots to show a panoramic view, or cutting to other scenes or characters can help to create these effects.

# Test your knowledge 7

**1** What is a review?

.................................................................................................................................

**(2 marks)**

**2** Name five things that might have a review written about them.

................... ................... ................... ................... ...................

**(5 marks)**

**3** Give three things you should do when reading a review.

a) ...........................................................................................................

b) ...........................................................................................................

c) ...........................................................................................................

**(3 marks)**

**4** State four things you should do when writing a review of your own.

a) ...........................................................................................................

b) ...........................................................................................................

c) ...........................................................................................................

d) ...........................................................................................................

**(4 marks)**

**5** a) What is a biography?

.................................................................................................................

b) What is an autobiography?

.................................................................................................................

**(2 marks)**

**6** What is the difference between the way biographies and autobiographies are written?

.................................................................................................................

.................................................................................................................

**(2 marks)**

**7** What do both biographies and autobiographies generally do?

.................................................................................................................

**(2 marks)**

**8** What does the term 'the moving image' normally refer to?

......................................................................................................................................

**(2 marks)**

**9** Give the terms which describe the following.

a) a shot showing the scene from a distance

......................................................................................................................................

b) a detailed shot of a character's face

......................................................................................................................................

c) a shot looking down on the scene from above

......................................................................................................................................

d) a shot looking up at something

......................................................................................................................................

**(4 marks)**

**10** Complete the following sentences.

a) Moving from one shot to another is called ......................

b) As well as images, films or TV programmes also contain ......................

c) Each image is called a ......................

d) A series of frames is called a ......................

**(4 marks)**

**(Total 30 marks)**

# Get organised

A basic, important thing that you need when writing is the ability to write in sentences. Sentences come in lots of different kinds – some are short and simple, others long and complicated – but they all follow the basic pattern shown below.

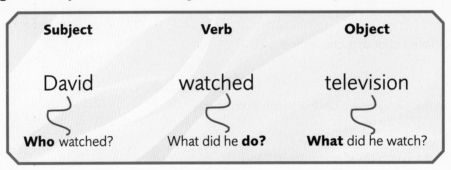

| Subject | Verb | Object |
|---------|------|--------|
| David | watched | television |
| Who watched? | What did he do? | What did he watch? |

Other important things about a sentence are shown here:

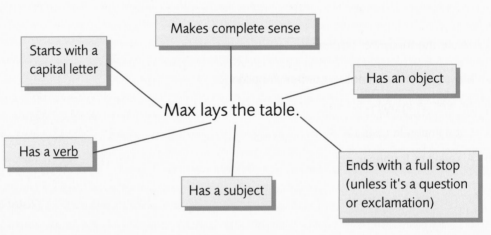

Starts with a capital letter

Makes complete sense

Has an object

Max lays the table.

Has a verb

Has a subject

Ends with a full stop (unless it's a question or exclamation)

Sometimes a good piece of writing can be difficult to follow if it is not organised in **paragraphs**. If you are writing more than a few sentences, work out how to divide your sentences into paragraphs.

Each paragraph should:

- have a separate topic
- begin with an indication of what it is about or what is going on
- develop this idea in more detail
- link with the ones before and after it, unless you move on to a completely different topic.

# A life sentence?

There are different kinds of sentences: statement, command, question, exclamation. Which kind is each of the following?

1 It rained heavily today. ........................

2 Are you going to the cinema tonight? ......................

3 Do as you are told. ....................

4 I hate homework. .......................

5 Get out of here! ....................

6 Come here now. ....................

7 English was really interesting today. ....................

8 Did you know that the trip has been cancelled? .....................

9 Call for me at 9.00am tomorrow morning. .....................

10 Robin, come down now! ......................

## KEY FACTS

A sentence always begins with a capital letter and ends with a full stop unless it's a question or an exclamation.

There are several different kinds of sentence:

- A statement tells you something.

- A command tells you to do something.

- A question asks something.

- An exclamation emphasises some kind of strong feeling like pain, surprise, anger.

Write in paragraphs for these reasons:

- It helps you to structure your writing in terms of dividing it up and organising it.

- This means that you need to **plan** out in advance what you are going to say and what each paragraph will cover.

- You need to think carefully about how your ideas link together from paragraph to paragraph.

- Paragraphs help to clarify the things you have written. A long section of un-paragraphed text is much more difficult to read.

## • TOP TIPS •

- **When writing, vary your sentence length and use a range of different kinds of sentences. This helps to make your work more interesting to read. Differing sentence length can help to set the mood of the narrative.**

- **Longer descriptive sentences create a sense of calm or a slow-moving pace.**

- **Short, sharp, clipped sentences – or even incomplete sentences – can make the pace more fast moving and urgent.**

# Where did you put it?

**As well as organising your work in sentences and paragraphs, you will also need to use punctuation marks to make the meaning completely clear.**

*It was Gala Day in the village and everyone was busy preparing for the procession that was to start in an hour – everyone, that is, with the exception of Jane's brother Tom, who was still asleep in bed.*

*'Hey. Get up you lazy lump!' shouted Jane up the stairs.*

*Loud grunting was followed by groaning, and then a croaky voice said, 'What's up? Is there something wrong?'*

*'Wrong!' shouted Jane. 'I'll tell you what's wrong. It's after twelve, you're still in bed and the parade starts in an hour.'*

See where the following types of punctuation appear in the passage above, and note how they are used.

- **Full stops** – A sentence always ends in a full stop unless it is a question or exclamation (question marks and exclamation marks also act as full stops).
- **Question marks** – You shouldn't have a problem knowing where to put question marks because they come at the end of every sentence that asks a question. (Your main problem might be remembering to put them in.)
- **Exclamation marks** – These are used after a word or group of words that express a strong feeling such as anger or surprise or to emphasise a point such as: 'No! Don't do that.'

Short sentences can give a sense of movement or urgency, for example:

*He ran as fast as he could. The mob were gaining on him. He feared he had no chance of escape. The end of the alley was there. No door. No gate. He was trapped!*

Longer sentences can often give a sense of slow movement , e.g.

*The boat moved slowly with the current of the river as it meandered its way through the overhanging willow trees that trailed their tips into the glassy water. Even the oars made no sound as they dipped and raised in a slow, unnoticed rhythm.*

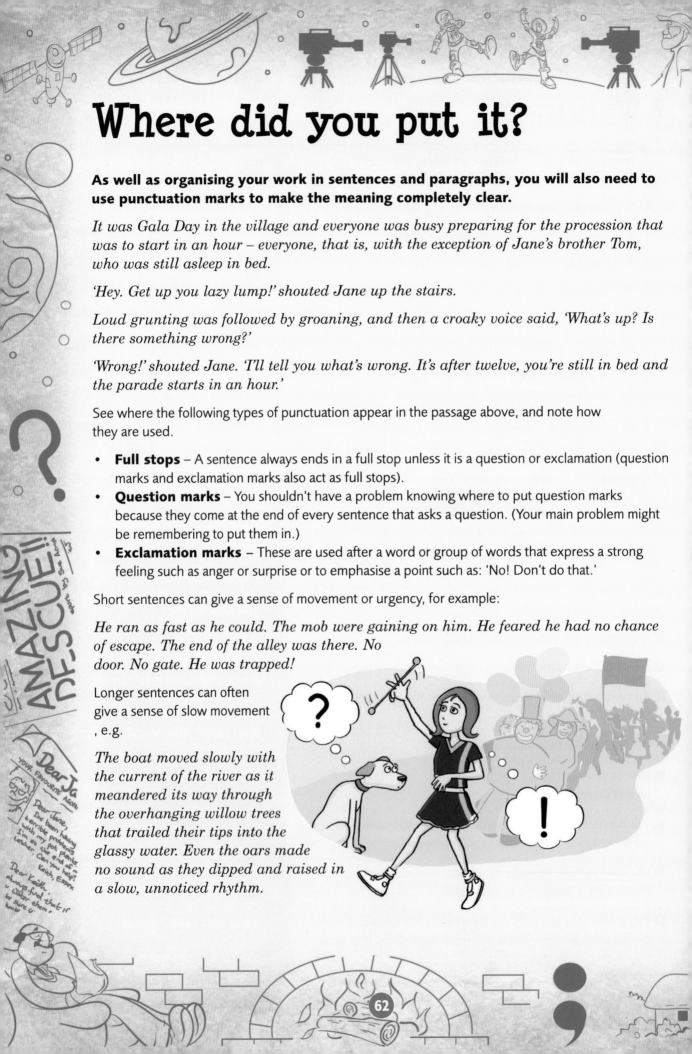

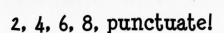

# 2, 4, 6, 8, punctuate!

Add either a full stop, a question mark or an exclamation mark.

**1** The teacher asked me why I was late

**2** What time does the film finish

**3** My friend asked me if I would help her

**4** Put that down now

**5** Could I borrow your DVD please

**6** What day is it tomorrow

**7** Hey, that's mine

**8** She wondered if I would go to the club with her

**9** Will you go to the club with me

**10** The singer asked if the audience would join in the chorus

## KEY FACTS

⬆ Always put a full stop at the end of your sentences unless they are questions or exclamations.

⬆ Indirect questions such as: *I asked him if he had enjoyed his birthday party.* should end in a full stop and not a question mark.

⬆ Direct questions such as: *Did you enjoy your birthday?* should end in a question mark.

⬆ Never use a full stop or an exclamation mark or question mark together.

⬆ Exclamation marks should be used for:

– emphatic comments

– strongly held feelings

– short expressions of strong feelings, such as 'Ouch!'

## • TOP TIPS •

How you use full stops, question marks or exclamation marks can both alter the effect and sometimes the meaning of what you are writing. Make sure that you use all three carefully.

# Who said what?

'Hey, did you see Chantal's mum on the telly last night?' Lee asked, 'She was going back to her roots – somewhere in Africa.'

'I don't believe it was her,' said Kelly, 'because I was talking to Chantal yesterday and she didn't mention anything about it.'

When you write direct speech you write down exactly what somebody said using the exact words that they used.

There are some simple rules to follow to make sure you punctuate your speech correctly. You use speech marks, also known as 'inverted commas' or 'quotation marks'.

Here are some different ways that speech can be punctuated:

*Anita said, 'I'm not bothered.'*

- In this example, the part that tells you who is speaking comes first, followed by the spoken part.
- A comma marks the part telling you who is speaking from the spoken part.
- The speech marks enclose the words spoken, and a full stop (or question mark or exclamation mark) comes at the end.
- The first word of the direct speech always begins with a capital letter.

*'Everyone stop talking,' said the teacher.*

- Here, the spoken part comes first, followed who is speaking.
- There is always some kind of punctuation mark between the actual spoken part and the rest – only a comma, a question mark or an exclamation mark can be used here.
- The speech marks enclose both the words that are spoken and the punctuation that goes with them.

*'Come on mum,' shouted Rachel, 'go down the water chute!'*

- In this method, two sections of speech are separated by the part telling you who is speaking.
- Notice how 'go' in this example begins with a small letter. This is because the sentence of direct speech has not ended yet.

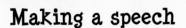

# Making a speech

Add speech marks and punctuation to these sentences.

**1**  Leroy's mum asked Where are your socks

**2**  You'll get much better value if you buy on the internet Sarah said

**3**  Do you want to know how to get there said Sam's dad Then look at the A to Z

**4**  Be careful! That concrete's not dry yet shouted the builder

**5**  The phone message said The only tickets left are £25 each

**6**  Are there enough chips here said Nicky or shall we buy some more

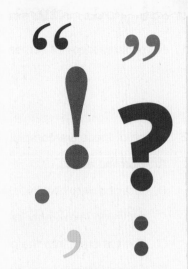

## KEY FACTS

⬈ Speech marks enclose everything that is actually said.

➡ The first speech mark goes at the beginning of the first words spoken.

⬇ The second speech mark goes after the punctuation at the end of the first words spoken.

⬆ When more than one person is speaking, every time a new person (or someone different from the last speaker) begins to speak, you should start a new line.

⬅ Never use speech marks when writing play scripts.

## • TOP TIPS •

Learn how to punctuate speech correctly so that when you are writing dialogue it is clear, easy to follow who is saying what and easy to understand.

Remember that speech reveals a good deal about your characters and how they relate to one another.

How you create their speech is an important element in making them convincing to the reader.

# Test your knowledge 8

1   Name three kinds of sentence.

    .........................................................................................................................

    **(3 marks)**

2   Which of these are complete sentences? Tick the sentences.

    A   Running away.

    B   It rained very heavily.

    C   Although I have only just met him.

    D   The cat crept into the garden.

    E   Coming from a large family.

    F   Having lost the first match.

    G   I felt happy at that moment.

    H   It was hot and she felt very tired.

    I   Tomorrow being Saturday.

    J   I hate maths.

    **(5 marks)**

3   What is a paragraph?

    .........................................................................................................................

    **(1 mark)**

4   Why do we use paragraphs?

    .........................................................................................................................

    **(1 mark)**

5   Punctuate the following sentences putting in a full stop, question mark or exclamation mark as necessary.

    a)   Are you coming out tonight

    b)   Ouch, that hurt

    c)   I asked if I could try it on

    d)   Do you think it will be hot again tomorrow

    e)   I don't know whether this is right or not

    f)   He closed his book quietly and smiled

    g)   I don't think I like this

h) Does it really matter that much

i) Quick, get down

j) He asked again if he could come in

**(10 marks)**

**6** Punctuate the following speech, putting in all the required punctuation marks.

a) Don't do that because it really annoys me said Kate

b) I think I'll wait until tomorrow said Sandra and decide then

c) It's a lovely present said Melanie

d) Hey shouted Mark I'm over here

e) I'm fed up with this homework said Ami and so I think I will leave it

f) Are you going on the trip to Holland too asked Tom

g) Toni asked do you have change for a ten pound note

h) What are you going to do about it demanded the woman

i) The teacher was cross and said do that work again

j) I'm not leaving said Helen until I get my money back

**(10 marks)**

**(Total 30 marks)**

# What's it called?

| Proper noun | | Common noun |
| --- | --- | --- |

James **ran** quickly for the **bus**, ~~pushing~~ through the **crowd**, but just as he **reached** the **road** he **saw** it **disappear** round the **corner** and **join** a long **convoy** of **traffic**. A feeling of **despair** **swept** over him as he **realised** that he would **miss** his **train** to **London** now.

**Collective noun**

**Verb**

**Abstract noun**

It is important that you understand what <u>nouns</u> and <u>verbs</u> do.

- Nouns are words that 'name' things such as people, places, objects, ideas etc.
- Nouns can be divided into several different types, each performing a particular function.

Proper nouns: the names of specific people, places, times, occasions and events, e.g. Jane, River Avon, Monday, London

Common nouns: the names of objects that we see around us, e.g. window, book, table

## NOUNS

Abstract nouns: the names of emotions, qualities, ideas and feelings, e.g. love, anger, bravery

Collective nouns: the names of collections or groups of things, e.g. flock, crowd, regiment

A sentence is not complete without a verb.

- Verbs express **actions**; sometimes they are called 'doing' words.

  For example:  The girl **swam** the length in record time.
  The crowd **cheered** their team.

- Verbs can also describe **states**; sometimes they are called 'being' words.

  For example:  Mary **is** very clever.
  Steven **seems** to be a rather nasty man.
  Liam **became** very interested in the subject.

# Naming, doing and being

**1**   Identify the types of nouns in these sentences.

a)   The **ball** bounced down the **street**.          . . . . . . . . . . . . . . . . . . . . . .

b)   **Robert** was very careful with his **books**.          . . . . . . . . . . . . . . . . . . . . . .

c)   The **band** marched down the **road**.          . . . . . . . . . . . . . . . . . . . . . .

d)   You could hear the **pride** in her voice.          . . . . . . . . . . . . . . . . . . . . . .

e)   You are a very generous **person**.          . . . . . . . . . . . . . . . . . . . . . .

**2**   Underline the verbs in these sentences.

a)   I telephoned you immediately.

b)   He drank the fruit juice quickly.

c)   I never thought that would happen.

d)   She ate her food slowly.

e)   The dog barked loudly.

## KEY FACTS

⬆ Nouns are 'naming' words.

➡ There are several different kinds of nouns.

⬇ Verbs describes actions.

⬈ A finite verb is one that has an object. In 'The girl fed her hamster,' the subject is 'girl', the finite verb is 'fed' and the object is 'hamster'.

⬅ The tense shows when the action of the verb takes place – past, present and future.

➡ 'Tense' refers to the way the verb changes its ending to express meaning in relation to the time at which an action takes place.

## • TOP TIPS •

In your writing, make sure that your verbs and nouns agree, and match plural verbs with plural nouns and singular verbs with singular nouns. For example:

• My cousin are due to arrive later. ✗
• My cousin is due to arrive later. ✓

# Imagine that

Alan is a **short**, **stocky young** man with **fair** hair and a **round** face.

In this sentence the <u>adjectives</u> give us more information about Alan. If the adjectives are taken out, the meaning of the sentence is lost: Alan is a man with hair and a face.

Using well-chosen adjectives can make your writing more vivid and interesting. Be selective, though, and only use adjectives which give the impression you want to create for your readers.

<u>Adverbs</u> tell us more about verbs:

- **where** something happened
- **how** something happened
- **when** something happened.

They supply the extra detail we need in order to imagine or visualise the incident being described, for example:

> He looked **angrily** at me.
> I walked **slowly** down the path.

Other adverbs such as 'rather', 'extremely', 'very' and 'nearly', can be used to tell the reader even more. For example:

> I walked **very slowly** down the path.

# Can you describe it?

1. Pick the correct adjective or adverb from the list to complete the sentences.

| torrentially | noisy | orange | very |
|---|---|---|---|
| violently | high | red | slowly |
| strong | deep | quickly | bright |

a) The ......................... sun set slowly in the west.

b) The man was ......................... in the face by the time he got to the top of the hill.

c) The ......................... party kept the neighbours awake all night.

d) The boy ran ......................... to school.

e) It was raining ......................... this morning.

f) Later the ......................... sun shone ......................... fiercely.

g) I awoke ......................... from a ......................... sleep.

h) The ......................... wind blew and the ......................... waves crashed .........................

2. Sometimes adjectives can be created from nouns. Write in the adjectives formed from the nouns.

| Noun | Adjective |
|---|---|
| Trouble | ......................... |
| Mountain | ......................... |
| Chaos | ......................... |
| Parent | ......................... |
| Giant | ......................... |

Some verbs can also be made into adjectives by putting one of the following endings on the verb: -ite, -ic, -ful, -ous, -ant -ive, -able, -y, -al

Change the following verbs into adjectives.

| Verb | Adjective |
|---|---|
| to sleep | ......................... |
| to explode | ......................... |
| to please | ......................... |
| to wake | ......................... |
| to love | ......................... |

## KEY FACTS

↑ An adjective tells you more about a noun.

→ An adverb tells you more about a verb.

↓ Well-chosen adjectives and adverbs help to make your writing more descriptive and so more interesting to read.

↑ Using appropriate adjectives and adverbs can help you to communicate your ideas more effectively.

· TOP TIPS ·

Beware of over-using adjectives and adverbs – this can make your writing sound forced, artificial or 'over the top'.

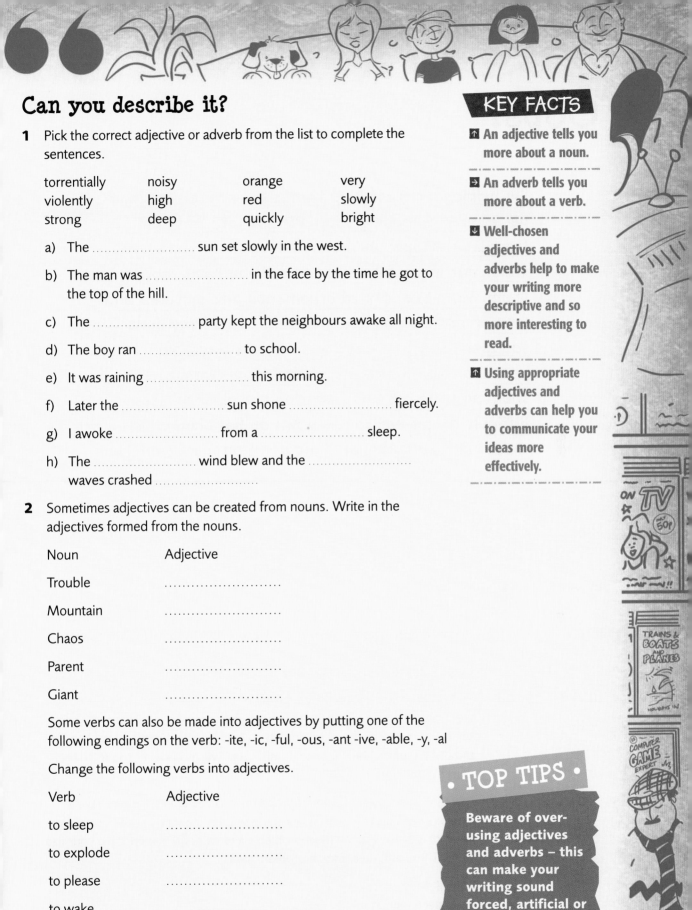

# Oops!

I'm helping mum pack up things in our maisonnette because were moving soon. We got lots of boxes from local shops, theres lots of room in some of them, but if you fill them too full you ca'nt move them. Mum has lots of ornements and pictures and lots of clothes she doesnt need. I said 'Why dont you give them to a charity shop, she says 'No because they remind me of the people who gave me them and the fun I had wearing the clothes'. Its difficult to get her to cut down on her things, so I expect Ill have to try and cut down on mine to show her how.

The account above includes some of the common errors that students make in their writing. As you read about errors below, look at the account again and spot examples of these errors.

| Error | Hints |
| --- | --- |
| Spelling | Doing more reading can help to improve your spelling, but in this revision period you can do other things too. Try making a list of all the words you frequently spell wrong and set yourself a certain amount of time to learn them. Try getting a friend or family member to test you on them at intervals. |
| Limited vocabulary | Try to vary your vocabulary by thinking of possible alternatives for words you use. Don't just rush to use the first word that comes to mind but think carefully whether it is exactly the word you want. Avoid going the other way, though, and using unnecessarily long or complicated words because you think they sound 'impressive'. |
| Punctuation | This can cover a whole range of problems and you are unlikely to have a problem with all of them. The first thing to do is to pinpoint the punctuation marks that cause you the most problems and work hard to improve your use of these. These are the common problem areas: |

- Full stops
- Speech marks
- Apostrophes
- Commas

# What's wrong?

Look carefully at the following sentences. Each has at least one thing wrong with it. Write out the correct version.

1  Charlotte left her bag on the bus

2  Simon and Toni enjoyed their sightseeing trip on the river thames although as they pointed out later it was rather expensive

3  Are you going now asked Kate. Yes replied David I've a great deal to do before tomorrow

4  This project is hard work said James. Not if you stop talking and concentrate smirked Rachel.

5  'Are you going to the meeting' asked Graeme.
   'Don't talk to me' shouted Debbie.

6  'Its going to be a long day if you two dont stop arguing,' said Mum. 'Youd think theyd be tired of it by now.'

7  'I wonder Mr Smith if you would mind locking up the hall after the guests have left.'

8  'Miss Haigh please make sure the children bring in eggs flour sugar milk and chocolate.'

9  he had a mean streak he always saw the worst in people

## KEY FACTS

⬆ **Always check your spellings carefully.**

⬆ **Make sure that you write in sentences.**

⬆ **Organise your work in paragraphs.**

⬆ **Know how to punctuate your work correctly using:**

  – full stops                  – speech marks

  – capital letters             – commas

  – question marks              – apostrophes

  – exclamation marks

⬆ **Know the functions of different kinds of words.**

➡ **Make sure that you use the right words to express what you want to say.**

## • TOP TIPS •

It is worth trying to get rid of basic errors from your work. It will improve your marks and make your writing more effective.

# Test your knowledge 9

**1**  What is a noun?

..................................................................................................................................................

**2**  Explain what the following kinds of nouns do.

  a)  common noun

  ..........................................................................................................................................

  b)  proper noun

  ..........................................................................................................................................

  c)  abstract noun

  ..........................................................................................................................................

  d)  collective noun

  ..........................................................................................................................................

**(4 marks)**

**3**  Identify each kind of noun.

  A  Shakespeare        ...............................

  B  river               ...............................

  C  queen               ...............................

  D  Queen Elizabeth     ...............................

  E  flock               ...............................

  F  table               ...............................

  G  jealousy            ...............................

  H  carpet              ...............................

  I  Monday               ...............................

  J  generosity          ...............................

**(5 marks)**

**4**  What is a verb?

..................................................................................................................................................

**(2 marks)**

**5**  Underline the verbs in the following sentences.

  a)  I telephoned you as soon as I heard.

  b)  The dog snatched the bone and ran away.

  c)  I wrote down the key points.

  d)  Walk, don't run in the corridor.

  e)  I packed my case and carried it to the door.

f) He swam strongly against the current.

g) I reluctantly swallowed the pill.

h) The man tripped on the kerb and fell over.

**(2 marks)**

6  What is an adjective?

..................................................................................................................

**(2 marks)**

7  Underline the adjectives in the following sentences.

a) The blue boat battered through the curling waves.

b) The tall, thin young man stood up.

c) The girl had blonde curly hair and a bright face.

d) The ghostly clouds floated slowly across the darkening sky.

e) The man lost his silver watch.

f) Bright lights could be seen shining in some of the windows.

g) The old man looked sadly at the broken gate.

h) The red and green parrot squawked very loudly.

i) Grey skies and pouring rain was forecast for next Saturday.

j) An old lady walked unsteadily down the rocky road.

**(5 marks)**

8  What is an adverb?

..................................................................................................................

**(1 mark)**

9  Underline the adverbs in theses sentences.

a) The cat sprang lightly onto the window ledge.

b) Walking slowly the prisoner emerged from the cell.

c) Sara wrote slowly but the minutes passed quickly.

d) I felt very sad when I heard the news.

e) You are being extremely rude today.

f) I nearly slipped on the wet floor.

g) The teacher smiled uneasily at the class.

h) I ran quickly to the bus stop but the bus pulled away.

i) James spoke quietly to his friend.

j) She sang poorly.

**(5 marks)**

**(Total 28 marks)**

# Glossary

**Adjective** – a word that describes a noun, e.g. 'red' in 'the red balloon'

**Adverb** – a word that tells you more about a verb, e.g. 'quickly' in 'he ran quickly'

**Advert** – a poster or feature in a magazine, newspaper or on television etc. that tries to persuade its audience to do something, e.g. to buy or believe something

**Advertising techniques** – these include particular language, visual or sound techniques that advertisers use to make their adverts more effective

**Alliteration** – the repetition of the same consonant sounds, e.g. 's' in 'silky smooth soft hair'. This technique is often used in advertising and poetry

**Assonance** – the repetition of vowel sounds in words, e.g. 'ough' in 'though the dough'

**Atmosphere** – the feeling often associated with a sense of place

**Audience** – the target group of readers or viewers that a text or programme is aimed at

**Caption** – a short passage of text that goes with a photograph or picture

**Close up** – in film, TV or photography, it is a picture taken close to the subject

**Cutting** – in film or TV, it is moving quickly from one shot to another

**Emotive** – this describes language designed to make the audience feel something

**Fiction** – literature that describes imaginary events and people

**First person** – a poem or story is in the first person if it is told by the writer using 'I', e.g. 'I had worried all day'

**Frame** – in film or TV, it is an individual picture

**Image** – in film, it is a camera shot: in printed advertising, e.g. in newspapers, it is a picture, illustration or photograph

**Imagery** – in writing, it is a picture created in words

**Long shot** – in film or TV, it is a shot taken from a distance

**Metaphor** – a comparison of one thing to another in order to make a vivid description. Unlike a simile, it does not use the words 'like' or 'as'

**Newspaper** – a daily, weekly or Sunday periodical that reports news and articles of many kinds

**Non-fiction** – writing that deals with things that are true

**Noun** – a word that names an object, e.g. 'window', or quality

**Novel** – a long, fictitious story published as a book

**Onomatopoeia** – the use of words whose sound copies the sound of the thing they describe, e.g. 'bang'

**Pamphlet** – a small booklet

**Personification** – attributing human characteristics to something not human

**Purpose** – the effect that a text is designed to have

**Review** – a piece of writing that gives an opinion on a particular subject, e.g. a book or a film

**Rhetorical question** – a type of question used for effect rather than to expect an answer

**Rhyme** – in rhyme, words contain matching sounds, such as at the end of lines of poetry

**Rhythm** – the 'beat' or sense of movement in a poem created through the stresses in the words

**Sentence** – a group of words that usually makes complete sense in itself and contains a subject, verb and object

**Setting** – the place or environment in which a story, play, film etc. is set

**Shot** – in film, TV or photography, it is a specific picture of the subject

**Simile** – a comparison of one thing to another to create a vivid description, usually using the words 'like' or 'as'

**Soliloquy** – a speech in a play spoken by a character alone on the stage – usually to let the audience know what is in the character's mind

**Syllable** – unit of sound

**Third person** – a poem or story is in the third person if the narrator is not one of the story's characters, e.g. 'he did this', 'she did that'

**Verb** – a word that describes an action, e.g. 'to run'

# Answers

## And your point is? (p5)

orange – offering an alternative
red – threatening disaster
green – rhetorical questions
blue – repetition
pink – use of exclamations
violet – emotive language

## Persuasive advert (p7)

1   exclamation – Amazing! Fantastic! Incredible!
2   repetition – Glide Easy
3   scientific-type language – integral, super turbo multi-angled
4   special offer – free accessories
5   emotive words – wonderful new hover cleaner, nightmare of vacuuming, a dream
6   guarantee – no-quibble money-back guarantee
7   rhetorical question – Fed up with pushing your heavy old vacuum cleaner around? Tired of struggling up the stairs with it? Frustrated when you can't get into those awkward corners?
8   status – Be the envy of your neighbours.

## How to look after your rabbit (p9)

bullet points - 5
advice on further information - 6
title - 1
introduction - 4
sub-headings - 2
imperatives - 3

## Do what it says on the card (p13)

1   explain
2   anyone interested in cooking
3   show the things you need
4   explain how to use them
5   clear and straightforward
6   structure the information

## Whatever happens next? (p15)

1   A        2   A        3   A
4   B        5   C        6   C
7   C

## Well, I think that... (p17)

1   Negative points – difficulty of providing good meals on a small budget; other demands on money in budget; students prefer burger and chips etc. to healthy food
    Positive points – young people's tastes can be changed; students can grow to like healthy options; healthy meals can be provided at a reasonable price
2   The article makes the comment that school meals must improve.
3   The writer is clearly in favour of healthy, improved school meals.

## What a story! (p21)

## I wandered lonely as a cloud (p23)

1   Alliteration          5   Repetition
2   Simile                6   Rhyme
3   Metaphor              7   Personification
4   Onomatopoeia

## What a performance! (p25)

1   To create a dramatic effect
2   urgency and tension
3   Give the audience information
4   witchcraft
5   Explain to the actors and director (and reader) what is happening
6   rhyming couplets
7   spell
8   magic

## Does it have to rhyme? (p29)

1   AABB
2   Rhyming couplets
3   Line 1 10, line 2 9, line 3 10, line 4 9
4   The beat of horses' hooves

## What is it like? (p31)

1   a red rose           5   eel
2   golf balls           6   rock
3   brush                7   beetroot
4   icicles              8   jet

## Crash! Bang! Clang! (p33)

1   assonance            3   onomatopoeia
2   alliteration         4   alliteration

## Building the structure (p37)

D, A, C, B

## What a guy! (p39)

| | | | ¹C | R | E | A | T | E | |
|---|---|---|---|---|---|---|---|---|---|
| | ²T | H | O | U | G | H | T | S | |
| | | ³A | C | T | I | O | N | S | |
| | ⁴P | R | E | S | E | N | T | | |
| ⁵R | E | L | A | T | I | O | N | S | H | I | P | S |
| ⁶D | E | S | C | R | I | P | T | I | O | N |
| | | ⁷O | T | H | E | R | S | | |
| | | ⁸D | E | V | E | L | O | P | |
| | | ⁹D | R | E | S | S | E | D | |

## Where am I? (p41)

A 4, B 5, C 2, D 6, E 1, F 3

## In my opinion... (p45)

Fact: 3, 4, 5, 7. Opinion: 1, 2, 6, 8

## What news today? (p47)

(word search grid)

## Can you believe it? (p49)

| ¹H | E | A | D | L | I | N | E | S |
|---|---|---|---|---|---|---|---|---|
| | ²A | D | V | E | R | T |
| ³C | O | M | M | A | N | D | S |
| | ⁴G | U | A | R | A | N | T | E | E |
| ⁵P | I | C | T | U | R | E | S |
| ⁶S | L | O | G | A | N | S |
| | ⁷G | I | F | T | S |
| ⁸C | O | N | S | U | M | E | R | S |

## What did you think of it? (p53)

1 CD player, 2 TV, 3 hotel, 4 vacuum cleaner, 5 novel, 6 meal

## Tell it like it is (p55)

| 1 | first | 5 | attention, interest |
|---|---|---|---|
| 2 | third | 6 | quotations |
| 3 | speech | 7 | information |
| 4 | thoughts, feelings | 8 | interesting |

## What a shot! (p57)

Crossword answers:
Across – 1 shot, 5 sequence, 6 close, 7 set
Down – 1 screen, 2 frame, 3 cutting, 4 reality

## Get organised (p61)

Statement – 1, 4, 7; command – 3, 6, 9; question – 2, 8; exclamation 5, 10

## Where did you put it? (p63)

1 The teacher asked me why I was late.
2 What time does the film finish?
3 My friend asked me if I would help her.
4 Put that down now!
5 Could I borrow your DVD please?
6 What day is it tomorrow?
7 Hey, that's mine!
8 She wondered if I would go to the club with her.
9 Will you go to the club with me?
10 The singer asked if the audience would join in the chorus.

## Who said what? (p65)

1 Leroy's mum asked, 'Where are your socks?'
2 'You'll get much better value if you buy on the internet,' Sarah said.
3 'Do you want to know how to get there?' said Sam's dad. 'Then look at the A to Z.'
4 'Be careful! That concrete's not dry yet!' shouted the builder.
5 The phone message said, 'The only tickets left are £25 each.'
6 'Are there enough chips here,' said Nicky, 'or shall we buy some more?'

## What's it called? (p69)

1 a) ball – common noun; street – common noun
   b) Robert – proper noun; books – common noun
   c) band – common noun; road – common noun
   d) pride – abstract noun
   e) person – abstract noun
2 a) telephoned      b) drank
   c) thought        d) ate
   e) barked

## Imagine that (p71)

1 a) orange
   b) red
   c) noisy
   d) quickly
   e) torrentially
   f) bright, very
   g) slowly, deep
   h) strong, high, violently
2 troublesome; mountainous; chaotic; parental; gigantic
3 sleepy; explosive; pleasant; wakeful; loveable

## Oops! (p73)

1 Charlotte left her bag on the bus. (full stop)
2 Simon and Toni enjoyed their sightseeing trip on the River Thames although as they pointed out later it was rather expensive. (capitals and full stop)
3 'Are you going now?' asked Kate. 'Yes,' replied David. 'I've a great deal to do before tomorrow.' (speech marks, question mark, commas and full stop)
4 'This project is hard work,' said James. 'Not if you stop talking and concentrate,' smirked Rachel. (speech marks and commas)
5 'Are you going to the meeting?' asked Graeme. 'Don't talk to me!' shouted Debbie. (question mark and exclamation mark)
6 'It's going to be a long day if you two don't stop arguing,' said Mum. 'You'd think they'd be tired of it by now.' (apostrophes)

7 'I wonder, Mr Smith, if you would mind locking up the hall after the guests have left?' (commas and question mark)

8 'Miss Haigh, please make sure the children bring in eggs, flour, sugar, milk and chocolate.' (commas)

9 He had a mean streak. He always saw the worst in people. (full stop and capital)

## Test your knowledge 1

1 a) A fact is a thing that is true.
   b) An opinion is one person's or a group of people's view or judgement of a particular thing.
2 facts – b, c, d, e; opinions – a, f
3 Capture your reader's interest and make clear your point of view
4 To emphasise your point
5 a) A question that does not require an answer
   b) To emphasise your point
6 Language that appeals to the emotions
7 To make points stand out clearly
8 To summarise the points made
9 a) purpose
   b) audience
10 stop, never, quiet
11 Options include – leaflets, magazine articles, posters, advertisements, internet sites
12 bullet points; clear and simple language; clear structure; the use of imperatives; indication of where further advice could be found; illustrations

## Test your knowledge 2

1 Writing to inform, explain or describe – B, C, F, K
  Writing to explore, imagine or entertain – A, E, H, I
  Writing to analyse, review or comment – D, G, J, L
2 a) storyline or plot
   b) convincing
   c) interest of the reader
   d) effective
   e) techniques, interest or attention
3 D, C, A, B, G, E, F
4 effects

## Test your knowledge 3

1 a novel or short story
2 a) say                    c) say about them
   b) do                    d) think
3 Capture the reader's or audience's attention and interest
4 The scene in which the action takes place
5 The ideas that run through the play or story
6 a) The use of words whose sounds copy the sound of the thing they describe
   b) The repetition of the same consonant sounds
   c) Corresponding sounds in words, usually at the end of each line of poetry
   d) The 'beat' or sense of movement in a poem created through the stresses in the words
   e) A comparison of one thing to another to create a vivid description, usually using the words 'like' or 'as'
   f) A comparison of one thing to another in order to make a vivid description (unlike a simile, it does not use the words 'like' or 'as')
   g) Describing something that is not human as if it is a living person
   h) The words that the writer uses
7 Read it through carefully.

8 The feeling often associated with a sense of place
9 a) build up a sense of tension or urgency
   b) give an informal impression
   c) make it easier to read
10 Stage directions tell the actors, director or reader where the scene is set, what the character is doing etc.
11 rhyming couplet
12 The sense of movement or beat of the lines
13 Include brief quotations from the text.
14 a) They leave (they exit)
   b) The way the writing is ordered or put together
   c) A speech in a play spoken when a character is alone on the stage
   d) A section of a poem (sometimes incorrectly called a verse)
   e) The storyline of a play or story

## Test your knowledge 4

1 Corresponding sounds in words, usually at the end of each line of poetry
2 The 'beat' or sense of movement in a poem created through the stresses in the words
3 A and C, B and D
4 Rhyming couplet
5 A comparison of one thing to another in order to make a vivid description; unlike a simile, it does not use the words 'like' or 'as'
6 A comparison of one thing to another to create a vivid description, usually using the words 'like' or 'as'
7 Simile – A, B, E. Metaphor – C, D, F
8 The use of words whose sounds copy the sound of the thing they describe, e.g. 'bang'
9 The repetition of the same consonant sounds
10 The repetition of vowel sounds in words
11 a) onomatopoeia          b) alliteration
   c) onomatopoeia          d) assonance
   e) alliteration          f) assonance
12 lines 1 and 2 alliteration, line 4 metaphor and personification, line 6 simile

## Test your knowledge 5

1 a) Capture the interest and attention of the reader
   b) By creating convincing characters and realistic settings
2 moving
3 Some kind of effect
4 planning
5 plan
6 effects
7 In any order:
   a) By what they say
   b) By what they do
   c) By what they think
   d) By what others say about them
   e) By how they relate to other characters
8 Because you haven't enough time or words to develop them properly
9 The background or situation it is set in
10 write from your own experience
   use vivid description
   make it realistic
11 physical description
   creation of atmosphere

## Test your knowledge 6

1  Things that are true
2  Things that people think or believe
3  Fact – B, C, F. Opinion – A, D, E.
4  To communicate news
5  A variety of answers possible, e.g. national, international, sports, political, human interest
6  Several possibilities, e.g. give TV programme listings, horoscopes, reviews,  etc.
7  To catch the attention of the reader
8  A sub-title given to a photograph or diagram
9  To help illustrate the article or capture the attention of the reader
10  layout, headlines, language
11  purpose, audience
12  newspapers, magazines, posters, leaflets
13  to persuade
14  headlines, slogans, photos, illustrations
15  repetition, exaggeration, promises, guarantees

## Test your knowledge 7

1  A piece of writing that gives an opinion on a particular subject, e.g. a book or a film
2  A film, a book, a DVD, a TV programme, a play, a computer game, a magazine, a holiday, a car etc.
3  Preferably in this order:
   a)  Identify the view being presented in the review.
   b)  Note how language is used to influence the reader.
   c)  Analyse the effect the review creates.
4  Preferably in this order:
   a)  Make it clear what you are reviewing.
   b)  Make your own view clear.
   c)  Give ideas or evidence to support the view you have.
   d)  Give a balanced view.
5  a)  A piece of writing about some else's life
   b)  An account of someone's life written by the person himself or herself.
6  Biographies are written in the third person and autobiographies are written in the first person.
7  Tell the story of someone's life
8  Film and television
9  a)  long shot          b)  close up
   c)  high-angle shot    d)  low-angle shot
10  a)  cutting
    b)  dialogue or speech or commentary
    c)  frame
    d)  sequence

## Test your knowledge 8

1  Question, exclamation, statement
2  B, D, G, H, J
3  A group of sentences or short  passage connected by theme or idea
4  To help structure our writing
5  a)  Are you coming out tonight?
   b)  Ouch, that hurt!
   c)  I asked if I could try it on.
   d)  Do you think it will be hot again tomorrow?
   e)  I don't know whether this is right or not.
   f)  He closed his book quietly and smiled.
   g)  I don't think I like this.
   h)  Does it really matter that much?
   i)  Quick, get down!
   j)  He asked again if he could come in.

6  a)  'Don't do that  because it really annoys me,' said Kate.
   b)  'I think I'll wait until tomorrow,' said Sandra, ' and decide then.'
   c)  'I think it's a lovely present,' said Melanie.
   d)  'Hey!' shouted Mark. 'I'm over here.'
   e)  'I'm fed up with this homework,'  said Ami,  'and so I think I will leave it.
   f)  'Are you going on the trip to Holland too?' asked Tom.
   g)  Toni asked, 'Do you have change for a ten pound note?'
   h)  'What are you going to do about it?' demanded the woman.
   i)  The teacher was cross and said, 'Do that work again!'
   j)  'I'm not leaving,' said Helen, 'until I get my money back.'

## Test your knowledge 9

1  A word which names something
2  a)  It names an everyday object.
   b)  It names a specific person, place or thing.
   c)  It names a concept or an idea.
   d)  It names a group or collection of things.
3  Proper nouns – A, D, I; common nouns – B, C, F, H; collective noun – E; abstract nouns – G, J
4  A word that describes an action
5  a)  telephoned, heard     b)  snatched, ran
   c)  wrote                 d)  Walk, run
   e)  packed, carried       f)  swam
   g)  swallowed             h)  tripped, fell
6  An adjective is a word that tells us more about a noun or a pronoun.
7  a)  blue, curling          b)  tall, thin young
   c)  blonde curly, bright   d)  ghostly, darkening
   e)  silver                 f)  Bright
   g)  old, broken            h)  red, green
   i)  Grey, pouring, next    j)  old, rocky
8  An adverb is a word that tells us more about a verb.
9  a)  lightly               b)  slowly
   c)  slowly, quickly       d)  very sad
   e)  extremely rude        f)  nearly
   g)  uneasily              h)  quickly
   i)  quietly               j)  poorly